D0211504

Crockery Cooking

Crockery Cooking is a complete collection of recipes especially designed for preparation in your slow cooker. Slow-cooked meals are the saving grace of many busy cooks, and the recipes included in Crockery Cooking are no exception. Taste bud tempting dishes such as Beef Bourguignonne and Down South Barbeque Pork are sure to be enjoyed again and again. Experience the savory tastes of slow cooking.

ISBN 1-57502-580-9

Recipe Compilation: Norma Guge
Editors: Dawn Feely, Tamara Omtvedt, Tara Harris
Cover Design: Erin Smith
Publisher: Scott Morris

Printed in the USA by:
Morris Press Cookbooks
3212 E. Hwy 30
Kearney, NE 68847
(308) 236-7888

Additional copies of *Crockery Cooking* may be obtained by sending a check for $5.95 plus $2.00 for shipping/handling to Morris Press Cookbooks at the address above. Order blanks are included in the back of this book.

Retail outlets may obtain *Crockery Cooking* at special rates. Write or call to the address above for more information.

Table of Contents

Slow Cooker Tips

Crockery Cooking Recipes

Note for the Reader:

Most of the recipes in this book use a
4-quart slow cooker unless otherwise indicated.

SLOW COOKING TIPS

The slow cooker – it's a tool found in most kitchens, but rarely used to its full potential. It is exceptional for creating effortless melt-in-your-mouth meats, thick, aromatic stews, and perfect vegetables. The slow cooker allows you to assemble ingredients the night before, turn it on in the morning, and return in the evening to a scrumptious, home-cooked meal.

Whether you are a beginner or an experienced cook, a slow cooker will enhance any meal. Dishes from appetizers to desserts can be easily prepared – you will soon create well-rounded, exquisite meals with just the turn of a dial.

Food Preparation for Slow Cooking

Beans
- Unless the recipe directs otherwise, dried beans must be softened slightly before adding to a slow cooker recipe. To soften, in a cooking pot, cover beans with three times their volume of unsalted water and bring to a boil. Boil 10 minutes, drain off water and add to your recipe.
- Acidic foods, such as tomatoes, and sugar inhibit the bean-softening process, so dried beans must be completely softened before combining with these types of foods. After boiling 10 minutes (see earlier instructions), reduce heat, cover and allow to simmer 1½ hours or until beans are tender.

Breads and Cakes
- Do not over-beat cake batter or bread dough—usually just beat 2 minutes.
- Use fresh, large eggs for the best bread and cake volume.

Meats
- Fat on meat can cause your dish to overcook and lose flavor in the slow cooker. Thoroughly trim all fat from meat and/or brown and drain it separately before adding it to the slow cooker.

Pastas
- Cook pasta until just tender before adding to the slow cooker.

Vegetables
- Thinly slice or dice firm vegetables; they cook slowly.

General Considerations
- Many recipes may be assembled several hours before cooking. Combine ingredients in a bowl, place in the crock, and refrigerate until you are ready to begin.

Cooking in Your Slow Cooker

Breads and Cakes
- After baking breads or cakes, cool five minutes, then invert the slow cooker on a cooling rack or platter.

Dairy Products
- Milk, natural cheeses, sour cream or cream should be added during the last hour of cooking to avoid overcooking and curdling.

Herbs and Spices
- Use whole-leaf herbs and spices to bring out their truest flavor in recipes. If ground herbs and spices are used, stir in during the last hour of cooking.

Meats
- When making roasts and stews, pour called-for liquid over meat. Use no more liquid than specified, because more juices in meats and vegetables are retained in a slow cooker than in conventional cooking.
- Do not thaw or cook large frozen meats such as roasts and chicken in the slow cooker unless you first add at least 1 cup of warm liquid. The liquid will act as a buffer between the food and slow cooker, preventing sudden changes in temperature. Cook recipes containing frozen meats an additional 4 to 6 hours on low or 2 hours on high.

Rice
- Uncooked rice may be added with other ingredients; simply add ¼ cup extra liquid per ¼ cup of raw rice. Use long-grain converted rice for best results in lengthy cooking.

Vegetables

- When preparing recipes containing meat and vegetables, add thinly sliced vegetables to the slow cooker first, as they take longer than meat to cook.
- When making a vegetable-roast dish, use a small amount of liquid to properly soften and cook vegetables.
- Small amounts of frozen vegetables may be used in a slow cooker as part of a recipe.
- It is not necessary to sauté vegetables before adding to the slow cooker; just stir them in with the other ingredients. However, eggplant should be par-boiled or sautéed, due to its strong flavor.

General Considerations

- Always cook with the lid on and resist removing the lid to check cooking food. Lifting the lid releases built-up heat essential for slow-cooked recipes. A slow cooker takes a long time to regain its needed level of heat; if the lid is lifted, cooking time must be extended.
- Do not preheat the slow cooker before using unless specified in the recipe. If the slow cooker has been preheated or is hot to the touch, do not place cold foods inside. Also, the slow cooker should be at room temperature before adding hot foods.
- Stirring is not needed while cooking on low. While using high, occasional stirring improves the distribution of flavors.

- Because there is no direct heat at the bottom of a slow cooker, fill it at least half full and follow recommended cooking times.

Recipe Adaptation

As you use your slow cooker to create wonderful, home-cooked meals, you may desire to adapt a recipe that was not originally intended for the slow cooker. The slow cooker can be used for many of these recipes with a few simple considerations. For delicious slow-cooked dishes, follow these tips on recipe adaptation as well as the tips in *Food Preparation for Slow Cooking* and *Cooking in Your Slow Cooker*.

Recipe Adaptation - cont.

- If a recipe calls for a specific liquid, you may vary the type of liquid as long as half of the original quantity is substituted.
- Use half the recommended amount of herbs and spices, especially if you use leaf or whole – the flavor power of herbs and spices increases during extended cooking.
- Soup recipes often call for 2-3 quarts of liquid. However, to compensate for the smaller size of a slow cooker, add all other soup ingredients; then add liquid only to cover. If thinner soup is desired, add additional liquid at serving time.

If recipe calls for:	Cook in slow cooker for:
15-30 min.	1½-2 hrs. on high or
	4-6 hrs. on low
35-45 min.	3-4 hrs. on high or
	6-10 hrs. on low
50 min.-3 hrs.	4-6 hrs. on high or
	8-18 hrs. on low

Proper Slow Cooker Usage

Setting
- The low setting on a slow cooker is about 200°F; high setting is 300°F.
- Low is recommended for slow all-day cooking. One hour on high equals about 2 to 2½ hours on low.

Safety
- Always use hot pads when touching your slow cooker while in use. All components will be hot to the touch after a few minutes of being activated.
- Do not submit the crock to sudden temperature changes; it cannot withstand these changes and will break.

Cleaning
- Don't clean your slow cooker while it is connected to an electrical outlet.
- Do not submerge your slow cooker in water.
- Use a non-abrasive cleaner to remove water spots and stains.
- After emptying food from your slow cooker, fill it with warm soapy water to easily loosen food remains.
- Use hot water to wash your slow cooker immediately after removing hot food. Do not fill with cold water if the crock is hot.

BEVERAGES, APPETIZERS & DIPS

BEVERAGES

HOT SPICED TEA

1 qt. water
3 sticks cinnamon
6 whole cloves
3 family size tea bags
2 c. orange juice
½ c. lemon juice

1 (46-oz.) can pineapple juice
1 c. sugar
1 tsp. almond flavoring
1 tsp. vanilla flavoring
Water (to make 1 gal.)

Place 1 quart of water in saucepan. Add cinnamon sticks and cloves. Bring to a boil. Pour over tea bags; steep for 5 minutes. Pour tea into gallon glass jar. Add orange juice, lemon juice, pineapple juice, sugar, flavorings and water. Keep hot in crockpot.

HOT WASSAIL

1 gal. apple juice
½ box brown sugar
½ jar orange breakfast drink
  mix
1 tsp. cinnamon

1 sm. can lemonade concentrate
4 c. water
1 orange
15 whole cloves

Mix apple juice, brown sugar, drink mix, cinnamon, lemonade concentrate and water. Put in crockpot and heat. Slice orange and insert cloves. Let float on top for added flavor. Will stay good all day.

CROCK-98

MULLED CIDER

2 qt. apple cider
1/4 c. brown sugar, packed
1/8 tsp. ground ginger
2-3 sticks cinnamon

2 tsp. allspice
2 tsp. whole cloves
1 orange, sliced (unpeeled)

Put apple cider, sugar and ginger in crockpot. Stir well. Cut a square of cheesecloth. Place cinnamon sticks in the middle. Add allspice and cloves. Bring up the corners of the cheesecloth and tie with a string, making a spice bag. Place spice bag in crockpot. Cut three slices of orange and float them in cider. Turn crockpot on high 1 hour before serving, then turn to low.

HOT APPLED CHERRY CIDER

3 1/2 qt. apple cider
2 cinnamon sticks

2 (3-oz.) pkgs. cherry-flavored
  gelatin

Mix together apple cider and cinnamon sticks. Heat on high in crockpot 3 hours. Stir in gelatin. Keep on high 1 more hour, allowing gelatin to dissolve. Turn to low to keep warm. Serve directly from crockpot.

SPICY CRANBERRY PUNCH

4 c. unsweetened pineapple
  juice
4 c. cranberry juice
1/2 c. brown sugar, packed
1 c. water

1 tsp. whole cloves and 1
  cinnamon stick, tied in
  cheesecloth
1-2 c. vodka (opt.)

Combine all ingredients except vodka in crockpot. Cover and cook on low 4 to 10 hours. Add vodka before serving. Serve hot.

HOT PEACH PUNCH

1 (46-oz.) jar peach nectar
1 (20-oz.) jar orange juice
⅔ c. light brown sugar

1 cinnamon stick
¾ tsp. whole cloves
1 T. lime juice

Combine peach nectar, orange juice and brown sugar in crockpot. Tie spices in cheesecloth or add loosely to punch. Cover and set on low 2 hours or on high 1 hour. Stir in lime juice. Turn to low to keep punch warm. Serve from crockpot.

APPETIZERS

HOT DOG SNACKS (EASY)

1 pkg. hot dogs, cut into bite-
    sized pieces
1 T. vinegar

1 T. maple syrup
1 (18-oz.) bottle barbecue sauce

Combine all ingredients in crockpot. Simmer on low 2 hours.

TANGY CROCKPOT FRANKS (EASY)

3 lbs. all-beef franks
1 (14-oz.) bottle ketchup

1 (18-oz.) bottle barbecue sauce
1 c. grape jelly

Cut franks into thirds. Combine ketchup, barbecue sauce and jelly. Pour over franks in crockpot. Cook on low 5 to 7 hours.

SWEET & SOUR FRANKS

1 (12-oz.) jar chili sauce
1 (10-oz.) jar currant jelly
3 T. lemon juice
1 T. mustard

2 lbs. franks, cut into bite-size
    pieces
2 (13½-oz.) cans pineapple
    chunks, drained

Combine chili sauce, jelly, lemon juice and mustard in crockpot; mix well. Cook on high 15 to 20 minutes. Add franks and pineapple to crockpot; cover. Cook on low 4 hours or on high 2 hours. Set on low to maintain serving temperature.

CROCK-98

EASY COCKTAIL WIENERS

1 jar currant jelly
1 sm. jar mustard

2 pkgs. wieners

Mix jelly and mustard together well. Cut up wieners and cook all on low in crockpot 5 to 6 hours.

CROCKPOT MEATBALLS

1 c. brown sugar
1 c. ketchup
2 T. Worcestershire sauce
2 lbs. ground beef
½ c. milk

2 tsp. salt
½ tsp. pepper
1 c. bread crumbs
Minced onion to taste

Mix sauce of brown sugar, ketchup and Worcestershire sauce and set aside. Combine ground beef, milk, salt, pepper, bread crumbs and minced onions. Shape hamburger mixture into balls. Bake at 400° for 10 minutes or until brown. Drain on cookie sheet with paper towels. Place in crockpot and pour sauce over. Cook on low 4 hours.

SWEDISH MEATBALLS

1½ c. bread crumbs
1 c. milk
1½ c. ground beef
2 eggs
1 c. onions, chopped
¾ tsp. dill

¼ tsp. allspice
⅛ tsp. cinnamon
1 (10½-oz.) can beef broth
¼ tsp. pepper
¼ c. light cream

Soak bread crumbs in milk for 5 minutes. Add ground beef, eggs, onion and spices. Mix well, cover and refrigerate at least 1 hour. Shape into 1-inch balls and place on cookie sheet. Brown under broiler, gently turning once or twice. Place meatballs in crockpot. Add beef broth, pepper and cream. Cook on low 4 hours or on high 1½ hours.

4

MEATBALLS IN MUSHROOM SAUCE

3 lbs. ground beef
3 eggs, beaten
2 lg. onions, finely chopped
1½ c. fine bread crumbs (plain)
1 c. milk
Seasoned salt & pepper (to
  taste)

3 lbs. fresh mushrooms
3 T. margarine
2 (10¾-oz.) cans mushroom
  soup
2 soup cans water

Put first 6 ingredients in a large bowl and mix thoroughly. Form into balls. Place on baking sheet and bake 20 minutes at 375°. Clean mushrooms thoroughly and slice. Sauté lightly In margarine. Put meatballs and mushrooms in alternate layers in crockpot. Add mushroom soup diluted with water. Cook on low 3 to 4 hours until thoroughly heated.

MEAT LOAF BALLS

¼ c. water
1 pkg. dry onion soup mix
¼ c. ketchup
¼ c. wheat bran
¼ c. oat bran
¼ c. dry bread crumbs
1 lb. ground beef
1 lb. ground pork
1 lb. ground turkey

4 eggs, beaten
1½ tsp. salt
¾ tsp. pepper
½ tsp. sage
¼ tsp. each: nutmeg, allspice &
  thyme
Water
1 beef bouillon cube

Heat water. Add onion soup mix and ketchup. Let soak 10 minutes, then add all other ingredients (except water and bouillon cube). Knead; shape into balls of 2 tablespoons each. Brown on each side and place in crockpot. Cover with water to which 1 bouillon cube has been added. Cook on low heat 2 to 3 hours.

BLACKBERRY BRANDY MEATBALLS

1 pkg. dry onion soup mix
2 lbs. ground beef
Crumbs made from 6-8 slices
  very dry bread

1 c. blackberry brandy
1 c. ketchup
1 (7-oz.) jar currant jelly

Mix soup mix and ground beef; add bread crumbs. Form into cocktail-sized meatballs. Fry; remove from pan. Drain and place in crockpot. Mix brandy, ketchup and jelly in frying pan. After sauce is blended, simmer until thickens to desired consistency. Add to crockpot and keep warm until ready to serve.

CHICKEN BBQ WINGS

3 lbs. chicken wings (16 wings)
Salt & pepper to taste
1½ c. barbecue sauce
¼ c. honey

2 tsp. prepared mustard
2 tsp. Worcestershire sauce
Tabasco pepper sauce, to taste
  (opt.)

Rinse chicken and pat dry. Cut off and discard wing tips. Cut each wing at joint to make two sections. Sprinkle wing parts with salt and pepper. Place wings on a broiler pan. Broil 4 to 5 inches from the heat for 20 minutes, 10 minutes for each side, or until chicken is brown. Transfer chicken to crockpot. Combine barbecue sauce, honey, mustard and Worcestershire sauce. If more heat is desired, add pepper sauce to taste. Pour over chicken wings. Cover and cook on low 4 to 5 hours or on high 2 to 2½ hours. Serve directly from crockpot.

WATER CHESTNUTS & BACON

2 cans whole water chestnuts
1-2 lbs. bacon (each slice cut in
  half)

1 (10 to 12-oz.) bottle ketchup
8 T. sugar
1 sm. jar peach baby food

Wrap chestnuts with bacon and secure with toothpick. Put on cookie sheet and bake at 350° for 30 minutes; drain. Transfer to crockpot. Mix ketchup, sugar and baby food. Pour over chestnuts and bacon. Cover and cook on low 3 hours.

PARTY MIX

2 c. O-shaped oat cereal
3 c. rice squares cereal
2 c. bite-sized shredded wheat
cereal
1 c. peanuts, pecans or
cashews
1 c. thin pretzel sticks (opt.)

½ c. butter or margarine, melted
4 T. Worcestershire sauce
Dash of tabasco pepper sauce
½ tsp. seasoned salt
½ tsp. garlic salt
½ tsp. onion salt

Combine cereals, nuts and pretzels in crockpot. Mix all remaining ingredients. Pour over cereal mixture in crockpot and toss lightly to coat. Do not cover crockpot. Cook on high 2 hours, stirring well every 30 minutes, then turn to low for 2 to 6 hours. Store in airtight container.

CHILI SPREAD

4 lbs. ground beef
3 c. water
3 cloves garlic, minced

1 T. salt
2-3 T. cumin
4-6 T. chili powder

Brown beef and drain. Put all ingredients in crockpot; stir thoroughly to mix spices. Cover and cook on high for 2 hours; stir well and turn to low for 6 to 10 hours. Serve topped with fresh, chopped onions. Try this over Mexican red beans.

DIPS

MEXICAN DIP

¼ c. melted butter
4 T. flour
1 tsp. jalapeño juice
1 heaping tsp. chili powder
¼ tsp. dry mustard
Dab ketchup

1½ c. milk
¾-1 lb. pasteurized processed
cheese, cut up
Garlic salt to taste
1 tsp. jalapeño peppers, finely
sliced

Combine butter, flour, jalapeño juice, chili powder, dry mustard and ketchup in double boiler. Cook until thick and bubbly. Add milk, cheese, garlic salt and jalapeño peppers. Stir until cheese is melted. Mixture should be thick. Keep warm in crockpot. Serve hot with plain tostada chips.

ENCHILADA DIP

2 lbs. ground beef
¾ c. onion, chopped
1 c. celery, chopped
1 lb. cheese, shredded

1 can cream of mushroom soup
1 can celery soup
1 can enchilada sauce

Brown beef; drain grease. Add beef and all other ingredients together in crockpot. Cook on high 2 to 3 hours, stirring occasionally. Serve with tortilla chips.

HOT CHEESE SALSA DIP

1½ lbs. ground beef
1 lb. pasteurized processed
  cheese, cubed

12 oz. salsa (6 oz. med. & 6 oz.
  mild)
White corn tortilla chips

Brown beef and drain grease. Combine cheese, beef and salsa in crockpot. Heat on low until melted, stirring occasionally. Keep hot for serving; use tortilla chips for dipping.

CHEESY BEEF DIP

1 lb. ground beef
1 lb. pasteurized processed
  cheese, cubed

1 can chili (no beans)
1 (12-oz.) jar salsa
1 bag tortilla chips

Brown ground beef and drain. In crockpot add cheese, chili and salsa. Stir in ground beef. Turn crockpot on high. Cook 45 to 60 minutes. Stir occasionally. Serve with chips.

MEATY BEAN DIP

1 med. onion, chopped
1 lb. ground beef
3 cans chili beans
1 lb. pasteurized processed
  cheese, cubed

2-3 shakes tabasco pepper
  sauce
1 lb. longhorn cheddar cheese,
  shredded
1 tsp. Worcestershire sauce

Cook onion with ground beef; drain. Add all ingredients to crockpot. Cook on high 1 hour, then low 1 hour with lid off. Stir several times while cooking.

CROCK-98

HOT REFRIED BEAN DIP

1 (16-oz.) can refried beans
½ lb. lean ground beef
3 T. bacon fat
1 lb. pasteurized processed
  cheese, cubed

1-3 T. taco sauce
1 T. taco seasoning
Garlic salt (as desired)

In skillet brown beans and beef well in bacon fat. Put in crockpot. Stir in remaining ingredients. Cover and cook on high about 45 minutes, stirring occasionally. Turn to low until ready to serve (up to 6 hours). Serve with warm tortilla chips.

Recipe Favorites

SOUPS & STEWS

CHICKEN

SOUTH-OF-THE-BORDER TORTILLA SOUP

1½ lbs. boneless chicken, cooked & shredded
1 (15-oz.) can whole tomatoes
1 (10-oz.) can enchilada sauce
1 med. onion, chopped
1 (4-oz.) can chopped green chilies
1 clove garlic, minced
2 c. water
1 (14½-oz.) can chicken broth
1 tsp. cumin
1 tsp. chili powder
1 tsp. salt
¼ tsp. black pepper
1 bay leaf
1 (10-oz.) pkg. frozen corn
1 T. dried chopped cilantro
6 corn tortillas
2 T. vegetable oil
Grated Parmesan cheese (for garnish)

In crockpot combine chicken, whole tomatoes, enchilada sauce, onion, green chilies and garlic. Add water, chicken broth, cumin, chili powder, salt, black pepper and bay leaf. Stir in corn and cilantro. Cover and cook on low 6 to 8 hours or on high 3 to 4 hours. Preheat oven to 400°. Lightly brush both sides of tortillas with vegetable oil. Cut tortillas into strips 2½ inches long and ½ inch wide. Spread tortilla strips onto baking sheet. Bake, turning occasionally, until crisp, 5 to 10 minutes. Sprinkle tortilla strips and grated Parmesan cheese over soup. Serve.

CROCK-98

CROCKPOT BRUNSWICK STEW

1 (2½ to 3-lb.) chicken, cut up
2 qt. water
1 onion, chopped
2 c. ham, cooked & cubed
3 potatoes, diced
2 (16-oz.) cans tomatoes, cut up
1 (10-oz.) pkg. frozen lima
  beans, slightly thawed
1 (10-oz.) pkg. frozen whole-
  kernel corn, slightly thawed
2 tsp. salt
½ tsp. seasoned salt
¼ tsp. pepper

In crockpot combine chicken, water, onion, ham and potatoes. Cook, covered, on low 4 to 5 hours or until chicken is done. Lift chicken out and remove meat from bones. Return meat to pot. Add remaining ingredients. Cover and cook on high 1 hour.

CHICKEN & SAUSAGE GUMBO

¾ lb. chicken breasts, cooked &
  shredded
½ lb. smoked sausage, sliced
1 c. onion, chopped
½ c. green pepper, chopped
¾ c. all-purpose flour
½ c. celery, chopped
8 c. water
2 cloves garlic, minced
1 bay leaf
1½ tsp. Cajun seasoning
1 tsp. salt
½ tsp. dried thyme
¼ tsp. black pepper
Dash of hot sauce
1 T. Worcestershire sauce
4 c. hot, cooked rice
¾ c. green onions, sliced

Brown sausage, onion and green pepper in skillet. Drain fat. In crockpot combine shredded chicken, sausage mixture, flour, celery, water, garlic, seasonings and Worcestershire sauce. Cover and cook on low 6 to 8 hours or on high 3 to 4 hours. Serve over rice and garnish with green onions.

CROCK-98

WHITE CHILI

1 (16-oz.) can navy beans,
 drained
4 (14½-oz.) cans chicken broth
1 onion, chopped
2 cloves garlic, minced
1 T. ground white pepper
1 T. dried oregano
1 T. ground cumin
1 tsp. salt

¼ tsp. ground cloves
5 c. chicken, cooked & chopped
2 (4-oz.) cans chopped green
 chilies
1 c. water
8 flour tortillas
Monterey Jack cheese,
 shredded
Salsa
Sour cream

In crockpot combine beans, broth, onion, garlic, white pepper, oregano, cumin, salt, cloves, chicken, green chilies and water. Cover and cook on low 8 to 10 hours or on high 4 to 5 hours. To serve, make 4 cuts in each tortilla toward center (but not through) and line serving bowls with tortillas, overlapping edges. Spoon in chili. Top with cheese, salsa and sour cream. Serve immediately.

CHILI CHICKEN STEW (EASY)

6 chicken breast halves,
 skinned, boned & cut in 1-in.
 pieces
1 med. onion, chopped
1 med. green pepper, chopped
2 cloves garlic, minced
1 T. vegetable oil
2 (14½-oz.) cans stewed
 tomatoes, undrained &
 chopped

1 (15-oz.) can pinto beans,
 drained
⅔ c. picante sauce
½ tsp. salt
1 tsp. chili powder
1 tsp. ground cumin

Put all ingredients in crockpot and cook on low 6 hours.

GROUND BEEF

BEAN HARVEST CHILI

1½ lbs. ground beef
Salt & pepper
1 can great northern beans
1 can pinto beans
1 can kidney beans
1 can navy beans

2 sm. cans whole-kernel corn
1 can condensed tomato soup
1 med. onion, diced
1 green bell pepper, diced
3 tsp. cumin
2 tsp. red chili powder

Brown ground beef in skillet, adding salt and pepper to taste. Drain off excess grease. Put all canned ingredients into crockpot (including the juice); stir until tomato soup is broken up. Add meat and stir. Mix in diced onion and bell pepper. After ingredients are mixed together well, sprinkle in cumin and chili powder; mix well. Cover. Turn crockpot on low and let it cook all day. Stirring isn't necessary. Serve alone or over cooked white rice.

EASY CHILI (EASY)

2 lbs. ground beef
2 onions, chopped
1 lg. can tomatoes
2 cans tomato sauce (or tomato soup)

2 T. chili powder
1 c. ketchup

Brown together beef and onions. Drain on paper towels. Put remaining ingredients in crockpot. Add beef and onion. Cook on low all day or on high 4 to 5 hours.

ZESTY CHILI

1 lb. ground beef
1 c. onion, chopped
1 lg. clove garlic, minced
1 tsp. dried oregano
1/4 tsp. black pepper
1 tsp. ground cumin
3/4 tsp. salt

1 1/2 T. chili powder
1 c. tomatoes, canned or fresh, chopped
1 c. tomato sauce
1 c. canned kidney or pinto beans, drained
1 c. water

Brown beef and onion; drain. Place all ingredients in saucepan. Bring to boil. Transfer to crockpot, cover and cook on low 6 to 8 hours or 3 to 4 hours on high. Taste for seasoning and adjust before serving.

HAMBURGER & VEGETABLE SOUP

2 lg. potatoes, sliced
1 (16-oz.) can peas
2-3 carrots, sliced
Diced onions
2 stalks celery, diced

1 1/2 lbs. ground beef
1 c. tomato soup
1 c. water
Salt to taste
Pepper to taste

Put all vegetables in crockpot. Lightly brown ground beef and pour over top of the vegetables. Pour tomato soup, water and seasonings over hamburger. Cover crockpot. Cook on low 6 to 8 hours or on high 2 to 4 hours. **Variations:** (1) Instead of hamburger, use diced turkey or chicken. (2) Use cabbage in place of onions. (3) Any kind of canned vegetables may be used to suit taste.

HAMBURGER MACARONI SOUP

1 lb. ground beef
1 can stewed tomatoes
1 can tomato sauce
1 sm. pkg. dry onion soup mix
1 sm. pkg. frozen mixed vegetables

1 can beef broth
2 c. water
3/4 c. elbow macaroni, cooked

Brown beef; drain. Add all ingredients except macaroni to crockpot. Cook 1/2 day on low. Add macaroni 15 to 20 minutes before serving.

SHIPWRECK STEW

1 lb. ground beef
1 can red kidney beans
1 med. onion, sliced

1 can tomato soup
3 med. potatoes, sliced
Salt & pepper

Brown beef; drain. Add all ingredients to crockpot. Cook 8 hours on low or 4 hours on high.

CABBAGE PATCH STEW

1 lb. ground beef
1 lg. onion, chopped
1 bell pepper, chopped
2 stalks celery, chopped
1 (16-oz.) can tomatoes
1 (16-oz.) can ranch-style beans

1 med. head cabbage, chopped
  fine
Water
1 tsp. chili powder
1/2-1 jalapeño pepper, chopped
  fine
Salt & pepper to taste

Brown meat, onion, bell pepper and celery. Add tomatoes, beans and cabbage. Put in 1/2 to 1 cup of water, depending on desired stew thickness. Add chili powder, jalapeño pepper, salt and pepper. Put all ingredients in crockpot and cook on low at least 3 hours.

BEEF & BEER VEGETABLE SOUP

1 lb. ground beef
1 med. onion, chopped
1 (12-oz.) can beer
1 (10½-oz.) can condensed beef
  broth
1¼ c. water
3 med. carrots, thinly sliced
1 med. turnip, chopped

1 stalk celery, thinly sliced
1 (4-oz.) can mushroom stems &
  pieces
1 bay leaf
1 tsp. salt
1/8 tsp. pepper
1/8 tsp. ground allspice

Brown meat and onion; drain off fat. Transfer meat and onion to crockpot. Stir in beer, condensed beef broth, water, carrots, turnip, celery, undrained mushrooms, bay leaf, salt, pepper and allspice. Cover and cook on low 8 to 10 hours or until vegetables are tender. Remove bay leaf and serve.

CROCK-98

HOMESTYLE HAMBURGER SOUP

1-1½ lbs. ground beef
1 med. onion, chopped fine
1 (28-oz.) can tomatoes
3 cans beef broth
1 can tomato soup
2 c. water
4 carrots, chopped fine
3 stalks celery, chopped fine

1 med. zucchini, diced
2 c. green cabbage, coarsely
  chopped
⅓ c. barley
2 T. parsley
½ tsp. thyme
1 bay leaf
Pepper to taste

Brown meat and onion; drain well. Combine all ingredients in crockpot; simmer on low 8 to 10 hours.

STEW MEAT

CROCKPOT VEGETABLE SOUP EASY

2 lbs. stew beef, cubed
1 (16-oz.) can tomatoes
2 carrots, sliced
3 stalks of celery, sliced
2 med. onions, diced
2 med. potatoes, diced

1 can green beans
1 can whole-kernel corn
3 c. water
1 tsp. salt
4 peppercorns
3 beef bouillon cubes

Put all ingredients in crockpot. Cover and cook on low 24 hours. Serve with cream-style cornbread.

WORKING WOMAN'S STEW EASY

1 pkg. stew beef (raw)
1 can cream of chicken soup
1 can cream of celery soup

Carrots, potatoes and onion (all
  raw & cut)

In the morning put all ingredients in crockpot. Cook all day. Needs no salt or pepper. This is great to make when you go to work in the morning; when you come home it is ready to serve!

HEARTY MAN'S STEW

Beef, cubed for stew
Onion, chopped
Salt & pepper
Potatoes, pared & diced

Water
1 jar spaghetti sauce
1 pkg. frozen vegetables

Brown beef and onions. Season with salt and pepper. Put potatoes in crockpot with meat and onions. Cover with water. Cook overnight on high. In the morning, add vegetables and spaghetti sauce. Turn to low.

SLOW COOKED BEEF STEW

1½ lbs. beef stew meat
1 med. onion, chopped
4 carrots, pared, cut into bite
   sizes
2 stalks celery, sliced
4 med. potatoes, diced
1 (28-oz.) can whole tomatoes

2 tsp. quick-cooking tapioca
1 (10½-oz.) can beef broth
1 tsp. Worcestershire sauce
2 tsp. parsley flakes
1 bay leaf
1 tsp. salt
¼ tsp. black pepper

Brown beef cubes. Put into crockpot and add remaining ingredients, stirring to blend. Cover and cook on low 8 to 10 hours.

NEW HAMPSHIRE STEW

1½ lbs. stew beef
4-5 med. potatoes, pared, thickly
   sliced
4 carrots, pared & chunked
1 env. dry onion soup mix
1 (6-oz.) can tomato paste
¾ c. water

¼ tsp. dry mustard
½ tsp. seasoning salt
1 T. Worcestershire sauce
1 T. bacon bits
¼ c. maple-flavor syrup
4 c. water
1 can peas with juice

Place beef in bottom of 6 to 8-quart crockpot. Cover with potatoes and carrots. In medium saucepan place all remaining ingredients (except peas) and cook until bubbly. Remove from heat and pour over meat and potato mixture. Cover and turn on high. Cook 8 hours. More water may be necessary. Add peas before serving. Do not thicken.

MINESTRONE

4 c. water
2-3 lbs. beef shank
1-2 lbs. marrow beef bones (2 or 3 bones), opt.
1 med. onion, diced
2 carrots, diced
2 stalks celery with tops, sliced
1 c. leeks, diced (opt.)
1 (16-oz.) can tomatoes
1 (10-oz.) pkg. frozen vegetables
2 tsp. salt
1 zucchini, sliced
1 c. cabbage, shredded
1 tsp. dried basil
1 clove garlic, minced
½ c. vermicelli or a 1-lb. can garbanzo beans
1 tsp. oregano
Parmesan cheese

Prepare stock a day in advance by placing water, beef shank and marrow bones in crockpot. Cover and cook overnight (8 to 12 hours) on low. Remove meat and bones from liquid. Cool. Scoop marrow from bones and return lean meat to stock. Pour stock into separate bowl and refrigerate. Later, add all remaining ingredients and 2 cups stock in crockpot. Cover and cook on high 1 hour, then on low 6 to 8 hours. Ladle into bowl and sprinkle with Parmesan cheese. Serve with crusty French bread.

VEGETABLE PORK SOUP

1 lb. pork stew meat or lamb stew meat, cut into ½-in. cubes
½ c. onion, chopped
1 tsp. paprika
1 T. cooking oil
1 c. potatoes, pared, cut into ½-in. cubes
1 c. loose-pack frozen whole-kernel corn
1 c. winter squash or sweet potatoes, pared, cut into ½-in. cubes
⅔ c. tomato, chopped
3 c. beef broth
½ tsp. garlic salt
1 tsp. pepper
1 c. fresh spinach, torn

Brown meat, onion and paprika in oil. In a crockpot layer potatoes, corn, squash and tomato. Place meat/onion mixture on top. Combine beef broth, garlic salt and pepper. Pour over mixture in crockpot. Cover and cook on low 10 to 12 hours. If necessary, skim fat. Stir in spinach just before serving.

19

PORK & HOMINY SOUP

1 sm. pork roast, cut into 2-in.
  cubes
2 cloves garlic, crushed
2 onions, chopped
5 T. chili powder

1 tsp. oregano
Salt to taste
2 cans hominy
Water (to fill crockpot)

Put all ingredients in crockpot. Cook on low until pork is thoroughly tender, 6 to 8 hours. Serve hot in deep bowls with toasted tortillas or chips on the side. Garnishes can be added to the soup according to individual taste: lettuce (shredded), radishes (sliced thin), hot pepper or cayenne, lemon or lime wedges, onions (chopped) and oregano.

VENISON STEW

Salt & pepper
2 lbs. venison stew meat, cut
  into 1-in. cubes
2 T. oil
3 stalks celery, cut diagonally
  into 1-in. pieces
½ c. onion, chopped

2 cloves garlic, minced
1 T. parsley, chopped
½ c. water
½ c. dry red wine
1 (8-oz.) can tomato sauce
1 (9-oz.) pkg. frozen artichoke
  hearts (opt.)

Salt and pepper venison cubes. Brown lightly in oil. Put celery and onion in crockpot. Add browned meat cubes and remaining ingredients. Cover and cook on low 10 to 12 hours or on high 4 to 6 hours, stirring occasionally. Serve alone or over rice or buttered noodles.

IRISH STEW

2 lbs. boneless lamb shoulder, cubed
2 tsp. salt
1/4 tsp. pepper
2 med. carrots, pared & cut in 1/2-in. slices
2 sm. onions, thinly sliced
3-4 med. potatoes, pared & quartered
2 c. water
1 sm. bay leaf (whole)
1/4 c. quick tapioca to thicken stew (opt.)
1 (10-oz.) pkg. frozen peas or mixed vegetables

Season cubed lamb with salt and pepper. Place in crockpot alternating layers of meat, carrots, onions and potatoes. Add remaining ingredients except peas (omit tapioca if you don't want gravy thickened). Cover and cook on high for 1 hour, then turn to low 10 to 12 hours. Add peas during last 1 to 2 hours of cooking.

VEGETABLE/CREAM

CHEESY VEGETABLE SOUP

1 (16-oz.) can cream-style corn
1 c. potatoes, pared & chopped
1 c. carrots, chopped
1/2 c. onion, chopped
1 tsp. celery seed
1/2 tsp. black pepper
2 (14 1/2-oz.) cans vegetable broth or chicken broth
1 (16-oz.) jar processed cheese

In crockpot combine corn, potatoes, carrots, onion, celery seed and pepper. Add broth. Cover and cook on low 8 to 10 hours or on high 4 to 5 hours. Stir cheese into crockpot. Cover and cook 30 to 60 minutes or until cheese is melted and blended. Serve. **Variation:** Omit the potatoes and chopped carrots. Stir in 1 (10-ounce) bag frozen mixed vegetables. Cover and cook on high 2 to 3 hours and then stir in cheese and continue to cook on high until well blended.

BEER CHEESE SOUP

2 cans cream soup (celery,
  mushroom or chicken)
1 c. beer or milk
1 lb. cheddar cheese, cubed

1 tsp. Worcestershire sauce
1/4 tsp. paprika
Croutons

Put all ingredients in crockpot except croutons. Cover and cook on low
4 to 6 hours or on high 2 hours, stirring occasionally. Serve in warm
bowls. Top each serving with crisp croutons. May be doubled.

CREAMY CORN CHOWDER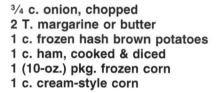

3/4 c. onion, chopped
2 T. margarine or butter
1 c. frozen hash brown potatoes
1 c. ham, cooked & diced
1 (10-oz.) pkg. frozen corn
1 c. cream-style corn

1 (10³/₄-oz.) can cream of
  mushroom soup, undiluted
2¹/₂ c. milk
Salt
Black pepper
Parsley flakes

Combine onion, margarine, potatoes, ham, corn, cream of mushroom
soup and milk in crockpot. Cover and cook on high 4 to 5 hours. Salt
and pepper to taste. Garnish with parsley flakes. Serve.

MEXICAN CORN STEW

1 c. dry pintos or other red
  beans
Water
1 tsp. olive oil
1 c. onion, chopped
1 T. garlic, minced
1/4 c. (or 3 sm.) jalapeño
  peppers, chopped
1/2 c. carrots, thinly sliced
1/2 c. celery, thinly sliced

2 red bell peppers, diced
3 T. cilantro, minced
6 c. vegetable stock or water
1 (16-oz.) pkg. frozen corn
2 tsp. cumin
2 tsp. coriander
1/2 tsp. cayenne pepper (opt.)

Cover beans with water, soak overnight. Drain and place beans in
crockpot. In a large skillet, over medium-high heat, heat oil. Sauté onion
and garlic until onion is translucent. Add jalapeños, carrots, celery and
bell peppers; cook 3 minutes, stirring frequently. Transfer mixture to
crockpot. Add cilantro, stock or water, corn, cumin and coriander. Cook
on low 6 to 8 hours, until beans are tender and stew is thick. Add
cayenne pepper, if desired.

CROCK-98

WILD RICE SOUP

1 c. raw wild rice
3 c. water
1 can cream of chicken soup
1 can cream of mushroom soup
1 can cream of potato soup
2 (4-oz.) jars mushrooms & juice
1 sm. onion, chopped & sautéed
1 lb. bacon, cooked & crumbled
8 oz. pasteurized processed
  cheese
1 pt. half & half
1 pt. water
2 med. potatoes, cubed

Combine wild rice and water in a covered baking pan. Bake in 350° oven for 1½ hours; drain. Combine remaining ingredients with the cooked wild rice in a large crockpot. Cook on low up to 8 hours.

FRENCH ONION SOUP

1 qt. beef bouillon
3 c. onions, thinly sliced
¼ c. butter
1½ tsp. salt
¼ c. sugar
2 T. flour
¼ c. dry vermouth
Toasted French bread
1 c. grated Parmesan cheese

Make bouillon (6 cubes per quart of water) and place in crockpot. Cook onions in butter in large skillet; cover and let cool 15 minutes. Uncover and add salt, sugar, flour and vermouth. Stir well. Add to bouillon. Cook in crockpot on low 6 hours. Serve in individual bowls with toasted French bread and cheese on top.

HOMEMADE POTATO SOUP (EASY)

6 potatoes, pared & cut into
  bite-sized pieces
2 leeks, washed & cut into bite-
  sized pieces
2 onions, cut up
1 carrot, pared & sliced
1 stalk celery, sliced
4 chicken bouillon cubes
1 T. parsley flakes
5 c. water
1 T. salt
Pepper
⅓ c. butter
1 can evaporated milk
Chopped chives

Put all ingredients into crockpot. Cover and cook on low 8 to 10 hours.

CROCK-98

LEGUMES

LENTIL SOUP

6 c. water
1 c. lentils, rinsed & drained (do not presoak)
½ c. barley, soaked overnight
2 slices bacon or ham, diced (opt.)
1 med. onion, chopped
2 c. carrots, sliced
2 stalks celery (with tops), sliced

2 cloves garlic, minced
1½ tsp. salt
½ tsp. pepper
1 tsp. oregano
1 bay leaf
1 can tomatoes
1 T. lemon juice or vinegar

Put all ingredients into crockpot; mix. Cover and cook on low 8 to 9 hours. When serving, sprinkle with grated Parmesan cheese and parsley.

POTATO & LENTIL SOUP (EASY)

3 onions, chopped
2 cloves garlic, minced
3 stalks celery, cut into 1-in. pieces
3 carrots, cut into 1-in. pieces

4 potatoes, diced
1 c. lentils
6 c. water
Soy sauce to taste
¼ tsp. paprika
¼ c. wine vinegar

Place vegetables and lentils in crockpot with 6 cups water. Cook on low setting for 8 to 10 hours or high for 4 to 5 hours. Before serving, season with soy sauce, paprika and vinegar.

CROCK-98

LENTIL-SAUSAGE SOUP

1 lb. pork sausage
2 med. onions, chopped
1 garlic clove, minced
2 c. lentils
1 T. salt

½ tsp. marjoram
2 c. cooked tomatoes or tomato
 juice
2 qt. water
Italian bread

Break sausage into chunks and brown. Remove meat and pour off all but ¼ cup drippings. Cook onion and garlic in drippings about 5 minutes or until tender. Combine all ingredients except bread in crockpot and cook for 9 to 10 hours on low. To serve, place a slice of Italian bread in soup bowl and spoon soup over bread.

HAM & BEAN SOUP WITH VEGETABLES

1 lb. dried navy or pea beans,
 presoaked & drained
4 c. water
1 (2 to 3-lb.) ham butt, cubed
1 onion, sliced
2 garlic cloves, chopped
1 green pepper, cut into strips

1 hot pepper, sliced (opt.)
1 carrot, sliced
Salt & pepper to taste
1 (10-oz.) pkg. frozen peas
1 (10-oz.) pkg. frozen lima beans
½ sm. head cabbage, shredded
Crusty French bread

Place all ingredients except frozen vegetables and cabbage in crockpot. Cover and cook on low 12 to 18 hours. Turn to high and remove ham. Add peas, beans and cabbage. Cook for 1 to 2 hours on high or until vegetables are tender. Serve large bowls of this thick soup with crusty French bread.

TOMATOEY HAM & BEAN SOUP

1 (16-oz.) bag mixed beans
Water
2 T. salt
2 qt. water
2 ham hocks or a piece of ham,
 cubed

1 lg. onion, chopped
1 (16-oz.) can tomato juice
1 tsp. chili powder
Pepper to taste

Wash bag of mixed beans. Place in a large kettle and cover with water 2 inches above beans. Add salt and soak overnight. Drain in the morning. Add 2 quarts water, ham hocks or ham and bring to a boil. Add onion, tomato juice, chili powder and pepper. Simmer in crockpot 3 hours on high or 5 hours on low.

OLD-FASHIONED BEAN SOUP

1 lb. dry navy beans, soaked
   overnight in water
2 qt. water

1 lb. meaty ham chunks
¼ tsp. ground pepper
1 med. onion, chopped

Put all ingredients in crockpot. Cover and cook on low 10 to 12 hours or high 5 to 6 hours.

NAVY BEAN SOUP

2 c. great northern beans
Water
1 ham shank, sliced
3 qt. water
1 c. celery, finely chopped
1 c. onion, finely chopped
1 c. carrots, finely chopped

Salt & pepper to taste
½ c. butter
4 T. flour
¼ tsp. ground oregano
½ tsp. dry mustard
¼ tsp. ground cumin
¼ tsp. chili powder

Sort and wash beans; cook in water in crockpot overnight. In morning, drain and add all other ingredients and cook approximately 8 hours more.

SPICY BLACK BEAN STEW

¼ c. water
1 lg. onion, chopped
2 med. red bell peppers,
   chopped
2 T. garlic, minced
1 stalk celery, diced
½ c. carrots, diced
¼ c. canned chilies, diced

1 tsp. cumin
½ tsp. coriander
3 c. fresh or canned tomatoes
1 c. tomato juice
1 (15-oz.) can black beans,
   drained & rinsed
3 tsp. chili powder (or to taste)
Salt & pepper to taste

In a skillet over medium heat, bring water to simmering. Add onions, bell pepper and garlic. Cover and steam 3 minutes. Spoon into crockpot. Add remaining ingredients. Cook on low 6 to 8 hours or until stew is thick. Salt and pepper to taste.

CROCK-98

SPLIT PEA SOUP

1 pkg. dried split peas
1 c. venison bologna, diced
½ c. onion, diced
¾ c. celery with leaves, chopped

1 tsp. salt
½ tsp. pepper
1½-2 qt. water

Put all ingredients in crockpot and turn on high for 1 hour. Reduce to low for 3 or 4 hours. Serve.

Recipe Favorites

VEGETABLES & SIDE DISHES

BARBECUE BEAN BAKE EASY

1½ lbs. ground beef
1 med. onion, chopped
2 (16-oz.) cans pork & beans
2 (16-oz.) cans butter beans
2 (16-oz.) cans kidney beans

1 c. ketchup
½ c. molasses
¼ c. brown sugar
2 T. Worcestershire sauce
3 T. liquid smoke

In a skillet cook beef and chopped onion until done. Put remaining ingredients in crockpot. Add meat mixture; mix well. Cook on low 3 to 4 hours.

RED BAKED BEANS

1 lb. red beans, washed
Water
1 can diced tomatoes
1 lg. onion, chopped

1 T. Worcestershire sauce
Creole seasoning to taste
1 lb. link sausage, cut up
Garlic

Place beans in crockpot. Cover with water until crockpot is approximately ⅔ full. (No need to soak beans overnight.) Add all other ingredients. Cook on low 10 to 12 hours. They will not overcook. May cook on high 2 hours, and then cook on low until done.

SMOKED BAKED BEANS

2-3 lg. cans prepared baked
  beans
1 lg. onion, chopped
1/4 c. ketchup
2 T. mustard
1/3 c. brown sugar

1/4 c. light corn syrup
1 T. tabasco pepper sauce
1 T. Worcestershire sauce
1 T. liquid smoke
1 bell pepper, chopped

Put all ingredients in crockpot. Cook on high 2 hours and then on low 4 hours. Serve as a barbecue side dish or with hot dogs.

BEAN & CORNBREAD CASSEROLE

1 med. onion, chopped
1 med. green pepper, chopped
2 cloves garlic, minced
1 (16-oz.) can red kidney beans,
  undrained
1 (16-oz.) can pinto beans,
  undrained
1 (16-oz.) can diced tomatoes,
  undrained
1 (8-oz.) can tomato sauce
1 tsp. chili powder
1/2 tsp. black pepper

1/2 tsp. prepared mustard
1/8 tsp. hot sauce
1 c. yellow cornmeal
1 c. all-purpose flour
2 1/2 tsp. baking powder
1/2 tsp. salt
1 T. sugar
1 1/4 c. milk
2 eggs
3 T. vegetable oil
1 (8 1/2-oz.) can cream-style corn

Lightly grease crockpot. In a skillet over medium heat, cook onion, green pepper and garlic until tender. Transfer to crockpot. Stir in kidney beans and pinto beans. Add diced tomatoes, tomato sauce, seasonings and hot sauce. Cover and cook on high 1 hour. In mixing bowl combine cornmeal, flour, baking powder, salt and sugar. Stir in milk, eggs, vegetable oil and corn. Spoon evenly over bean mixture. May have leftover cornbread, depending on size of crockpot being used (if have remaining cornbread, spoon into greased muffin tins and bake at 375° for 30 minutes or until golden brown). Cover and cook on high for 1 1/2 to 2 more hours. Serve.

CROCK-98

EASY PINTO BEANS

1 lb. pinto beans
1 can stewed tomatoes
1 sm. can tomato sauce

½ onion, chopped
Salt pork, diced
Sm. bunch cilantro

Combine all ingredients and put in crockpot. Cook overnight or 8 to 10 hours.

CROCKPOT POTATOES

1 (2-lb.) pkg. frozen hash
  browns
½ pt. sour cream
Few green onions, cut up
1 (8-oz.) pkg. pasteurized
  processed cheese, cut in sm.
  pieces

1 can cream of chicken soup
Salt & pepper

Put all ingredients in crockpot. Stir well and occasionally while cooking. Cook on low 6 to 8 hours, or high 4 to 5 hours.

SCALLOPED POTATOES

8 lg. potatoes, pared & sliced
½ c. margarine (in stick)
½ c. onions, chopped
⅓ c. flour

2 tsp. salt
¼ tsp. pepper
3 c. milk

Place potatoes in bottom of crockpot. Slice stick of margarine and spread over top of potatoes. Layer onions on top of margarine. Sprinkle flour, salt and pepper over onions. Pour milk over all. Cook on low for at least 2 hours. Stir occasionally.

HOT GERMAN POTATO SALAD

½ lb. bacon
½ c. onion, chopped
2 T. flour
2 T. sugar
1½ tsp. salt

1 tsp. celery seed
½ c. vinegar (apple cider)
6 c. cooked potatoes, diced
2 hard-cooked eggs, diced

Cook bacon in large skillet until crisp; drain, reserving fat, crumble and set aside. Cook onion in bacon fat until tender. Blend in flour, sugar, salt, celery seed and vinegar. Stir until thick and bubbly. Add potatoes, bacon and eggs. Heat thoroughly, tossing lightly. Pour into crockpot and keep on low until ready to serve. If desired, garnish with parsley, pimento or bacon curls.

CHEESY CROCKPOT POTATOES

2½ lbs. pasteurized processed
  cheese
1 c. cheddar cheese, shredded

1 c. butter
2 lg. bags hash browns
1 pt. half & half

Melt cheeses and butter together. Put potatoes in crockpot. Pour cheese and half & half together over potatoes. Let sit 1 hour. Turn on high 1 hour, then cook on low 2 hours. May need to cook longer. Potatoes are done when soft and all liquid has been absorbed.

BAKING POTATOES
OR SWEET POTATOES

Wash potatoes thoroughly. Wrap in foil. Place in crockpot and put on low for 8 to 10 hours. Make as many potatoes as you need.

EASY CROCKPOT POTATOES

1 (2-lb.) bag au gratin potatoes
2 (10-oz.) cans cheddar cheese
  soup

1 (13-oz.) can evaporated milk
1 can French-fried onion rings
Salt & pepper

Grease crockpot. Mix all ingredients, reserving half of the onion rings. Place in crockpot; garnish with onion rings. Cook on low 8 to 9 hours or on high 4 hours.

GREEN BEAN CASSEROLE

1 pkg. frozen French-style green beans
1 can cream of mushroom soup
1½ c. milk
1 pkg. frozen onion rings
Slivered almonds (opt.)

Steam beans. Put in crockpot. Add soup, milk, onion rings and slivered almonds. Cook on low 8 hours.

CHEESY GREEN BEAN CASSEROLE

2 lbs. fresh green beans, washed & cut up
1 (10½-oz.) can cream of mushroom soup (undiluted)
1 can French-fried onion rings
1 c. cheddar cheese, grated
1 can water chestnuts, thinly sliced
Slivered almonds (opt.)
Salt & pepper to taste
½ c. water

Spread all ingredients, except water, in layers as listed above, in crockpot, making about three layers. Save enough onion rings to crumble and sprinkle over top about 20 minutes before serving. Add water and cook on high 7 to 10 hours, or on low 12 to 18 hours. **Note:** If using frozen green beans, use 4 packages cut-up. Cook on low 8 to 10 hours or on high 4 to 5 hours.

BBQ GREEN BEANS

4 slices bacon, diced
1 med. onion, diced
1 c. brown sugar
1 c. ketchup
4 cans green beans

Brown bacon and onion; drain well. Add sugar and ketchup. Simmer 5 minutes. Drain beans and put in crockpot. Pour sauce over beans. Bake on low 4 hours.

FRESH GREEN BEANS

4 lbs. fresh green beans, washed & cut up
3-4 c. water
1 tsp. salt
¼ lb. ham or bacon pieces

Put all ingredients in crockpot. Cover and cook on low 10 to 24 hours or on high 6 to 10 hours. Stir occasionally.

FRESH CORN ON THE COB

Remove corn silks but leave green outer husks on the ears and cut off ends so 6 to 8 ears will fit in crockpot in standing position. Wash thoroughly. Cover and cook on high 45 minutes, then turn to low for 1½ to 2 hours. Remove husks and serve.

CREAMY CORN

2 (16-oz.) cans whole-kernel
  corn, drained
4 oz. cream cheese, cubed

2-4 T. butter
½-1 tsp. garlic salt

Mix all ingredients together. Place in crockpot. Cook on low 2 to 3 hours.

ACORN SQUASH (EASY)

Acorn squash
Salt

Cinnamon
Butter

Place whole rinsed squash in crockpot. Cook on low 8 to 10 hours. Split and remove seeds when cooked. Sprinkle with salt and cinnamon and dot with butter. (May be split and wrapped with foil before baking.)

ARTICHOKES

4-6 artichokes
Salt
Lemon juice

2 c. hot water
Melted butter & lemon juice or
  Sauterne Sauce

Wash and trim artichokes. Cut off about 1 inch from top. If desired, trim tips of leaves. Stand upright in crockpot. Add ¼ teaspoon salt for each artichoke and 2 tablespoons lemon juice. Pour in water. Cover and cook on low 6 to 8 hours. Serve with melted butter and lemon or Sauterne Sauce.

Sauterne Sauce:

1 c. sauterne
3 T. minced onion
2 c. mayonnaise

3 T. parsley flakes
3 T. lemon juice
1 egg, beaten

Mix all sauce ingredients and heat slowly. Dip artichoke leaves and hearts into sauce.

CROCK-98

BAVARIAN RED CABBAGE (EASY)

1 sm. head red cabbage,
  washed & coarsely sliced
1 med. onion, chopped
3 tart apples, cored & quartered
2 tsp. salt

1 c. hot water
1½ T. sugar
½ c. vinegar
3 T. butter

Place all ingredients in crockpot in order listed. Cover and cook on low 8 to 10 hours or on high 3 hours. Stir well before serving.

SWEET & SOUR RED CABBAGE

4 slices bacon, diced
3 T. brown sugar
2 T. flour
½ tsp. salt
Pepper

½ c. water
¼ c. vinegar
1 sm./med. head red cabbage,
  shredded (6-8 c.)
1 onion, finely chopped

Cook bacon in skillet. Put bacon and 1 tablespoon drippings in crockpot with sugar, flour, salt and pepper. Stir in water and vinegar. Add cabbage and onion. Cover and cook on low 3 to 4 hours.

CARROTS JULIENNE

1 chicken bouillon cube
1 c. boiling water
2 onions, diced
¼ c. butter or margarine

1 T. flour
¼ tsp. salt
6 carrots, pared & julienned

Dissolve bouillon cube in boiling water; set aside. In large skillet sauté onions in butter. Stir flour and salt into slightly cooled bouillon; add to onions and cook until thickened. Combine carrots and onion sauce in crockpot, stirring to coat carrots. Cover and cook on high 1 hour, then turn to low 2 to 6 hours.

BROCCOLI CASSEROLE

2 (10-oz.) pkgs. frozen broccoli
  spears, thawed & cut up
1 (10³/₄-oz.) can condensed
  cream of celery soup

1¼ c. sharp cheddar cheese,
  grated
¼ c. green onion, minced
1 c. saltine crackers, crushed

In large bowl combine broccoli, celery soup, 1 cup of grated cheese and minced onion. Pour into lightly greased crockpot. Sprinkle top with crackers, then with remaining cheese. Cover and cook on low 5 to 6 hours or on high 2½ to 3 hours.

SPINACH CASSEROLE

2 (10-oz.) pkgs. frozen spinach,
  thawed, chopped & drained
2 c. cream-style cottage cheese
½ c. butter, cut into pieces

1½ c. American cheese, cubed
3 eggs, beaten
¼ c. flour
1 tsp. salt

Thoroughly combine all ingredients in mixing bowl. Pour into greased crockpot. Cover and cook on high 1 hour, then turn to low for 4 to 5 hours.

SOUTHERN-STYLE BLACK-EYED PEAS

1 lb. dried black-eyed peas
4 c. water
2 tsp. salt
¼ tsp. pepper

1 lg. onion, chopped
2 stalks celery, chopped (opt.)
½ lb. salt pork, sliced (or 2 ham
  hocks)

Soak peas in water overnight. Drain and place in crockpot. Add remaining ingredients. Cover and cook on high 1 to 2 hours, then turn to low for 8 to 9 hours. Serve over fluffy hot rice with cornbread. **Note:** 3 packages frozen black-eyed peas may be substituted for dried peas. Use only 2 cups water.

CROCK-98

GOURMET DRESSING

1 lg. onion
2 cloves garlic
2 stalks celery
1 green pepper
1 (8-oz.) pkg. chicken livers or 2
  slices beef liver (opt.)
2 tsp. salt

½ tsp. pepper
2-3 bay leaves
1 lb. ground beef
10-12 oz. fresh or frozen oysters
2 c. rice
4 c. water

Grind onion, garlic, celery and green pepper with chicken or beef liver; add salt and pepper to taste. Mix in whole bay leaves; combine all with ground beef. Lightly oil skillet and bring to medium heat (not hot). Cook meat mixture slowly until meat is well cooked, stirring occasionally (it may be necessary to add a little water). Grind oysters and place in separate bowl. Place rice, water and 1 teaspoon salt in saucepan; bring to boil. Simmer, covered, until water is boiled out and rice grains separate (about 30 minutes). Combine all thoroughly and place into lightly greased crockpot. Cover and cook on low 4 to 6 hours. As a casserole side dish — great with all game or rich meats.

RICE PILAF (EASY)

1 (10½-oz.) can beef broth
1 (4-oz.) can sliced mushrooms,
  drained

½ c. raw converted rice
2 T. butter or margarine
⅓ c. onion, finely chopped

Put all ingredients in crockpot. Cover and cook 6 to 8 hours.

SCRUMPTIOUS STUFFING

1 c. onion, chopped
1 c. celery, chopped
¾ c. margarine
1 (1-lb.) loaf plus 8 slices bread,
  cubed
1 tsp. baking powder

2½ tsp. sage
½ tsp. pepper
2 (10¾-oz.) cans cream of
  chicken soup
1 (10½-oz.) can chicken broth
4 eggs, beaten
2 apples, diced

Spray crockpot with nonstick cooking spray. Sauté onion and celery in margarine. Mix all ingredients and place in crockpot. Cook on high 1 hour. Turn down to low and continue cooking 5 hours.

YUMMY MACARONI & CHEESE

3 c. sharp cheddar cheese,
  grated
1 lg. can evaporated milk
1½ c. milk
3 eggs, slightly beaten
¼ c. butter, melted

2 T. oil
1 tsp. salt
1 (8-oz.) box macaroni,
  cooked & drained

Combine all ingredients and put in a well-greased crockpot. Add extra cheese slices on top, if desired. Cook on low 4 hours.

BEEF COOKERY

ROASTS

BEEF AU JUS

2 lg. onions
¼ c. butter
½ c. soy sauce
1 clove garlic, minced

5 c. water
3 to 4-lb. beef roast (rump,
   bottom round or brisket)

Brown onions in butter. Add soy sauce, garlic and water. Put roast in crockpot and add liquid. Cover and cook 8 to 10 hours on low. Slice roast after cooled and put back in liquid to serve.

POT ROAST WITH MUSHROOMS

Pot roast
2 T. brown sugar
2 T. ketchup
1 sm. onion, chopped

Fresh mushrooms
1 pkg. dry onion soup mix
1 lg. carton sour cream

Cover roast with mixture of brown sugar and ketchup. Layer on chopped onion and mushrooms. Mix one envelope of soup mix with sour cream and cover roast with it. Cook on high in crockpot for 5 hours or until meat is tender and falls apart.

CROCK-98

MARINATED CHUCK

Meat tenderizer
Chuck roast
5 T. soy sauce
3 T. vinegar
3 T. water
Dash of liquid smoke

Dash of Worcestershire sauce
1/2 tsp. ginger
1/2 tsp. garlic powder
Dash of salt & pepper
1/2 tsp. sugar

Tenderize chuck roast. Mix all remaining ingredients and pour over meat. Marinate 4 hours before cooking. Cook in crockpot on low all day.

COUNTRY BRISKET

6-lb. brisket
1 T. garlic salt
1 T. pepper
2 sm. onions, sliced

1 c. chili sauce
1 T. celery seed
1 T. mustard powder or seed

Sprinkle meat with garlic salt and pepper. Arrange onions in bottom of crockpot. Place meat on top. Combine chili sauce, celery seed and mustard; pour over meat. Cook on low 10 to 12 hours until tender.

DILLED POT ROAST

Potatoes, cubed
1/2 tsp. salt
1/4 tsp. pepper
1 tsp. dill weed
1/2 tsp. minced garlic

3 to 3 1/2-lb. beef pot roast
Onion, quartered
Carrots, peeled & cut up
1/4 c. water

Put potatoes in bottom of crockpot. Sprinkle mixture of all spices on beef roast. Place roast on top of potatoes. Add onions and carrots. Add water. Cover and cook on low 7 to 9 hours or until tender.

CROCK-98

BEEF ROAST & VEGETABLES (EASY)

3 lbs. beef roast
6 lg. potatoes, pared &
 quartered
2 lg. onions, peeled & quartered

1 lb. carrots, pared & diced
1 tsp. pepper
1 tsp. garlic powder
1 pkg. dry onion soup mix

Place roast in crockpot. Add vegetables, pepper, garlic powder and soup mix. Cook on low 6 to 8 hours.

PAPA'S POT ROAST

3-4 lbs. beef rump or chuck
 roast
1 tsp. salt
$\frac{1}{2}$ tsp. seasoned salt
$\frac{1}{4}$ tsp. seasoned pepper

$\frac{1}{4}$ tsp. paprika
1 T. onion, chopped
1 c. beef bouillon
Vegetables as desired

Rub all sides of meat with seasonings. Place in crockpot with onion and bouillon. Cover and cook on low 8 to 10 hours, or until meat is tender. Vegetables, such as potatoes, carrots, small onions, celery or turnips, may be cooked with meat and juice about $1\frac{1}{2}$ hours before meat is done. Thicken gravy with flour and water.

MELT-IN-YOUR-MOUTH POT ROAST

2-3 potatoes, pared & diced
2-3 carrots, pared & diced
1-2 onions, peeled & diced
Salt & pepper to taste

3 to 4-lb. beef brisket, rump
 roast or pot roast
$\frac{1}{2}$ c. water or beef consomme

Put half of vegetables in bottom of crockpot. Salt and pepper meat, then put in pot. Add remaining vegetables, liquid and salt and pepper. Cover and cook on low 10 to 12 hours or on high 5 to 6 hours. Remove meat and vegetables with spatula and serve.

CROCK-98

CROCKPOT ROAST DELUXE

3-4 potatoes, pared & quartered
4-6 onions, halved
3 to 6-lb. chuck roast
Salt & pepper to taste

1 can tomato soup
1 c. water
1 (4-oz.) can mushrooms
  stems & pieces

Place potatoes and onions in crockpot. Add roast, salt and pepper. Pour soup over top. Add 1 cup water. Arrange mushrooms over top. Cover and cook on low 8 to 10 hours or on high 4 to 6 hours.

RANCH-STYLE ROAST

1 beef roast (any cut)
1 can cream of mushroom soup
1 c. red wine
1 pkg. Ranch-style dressing
  (dry)

1-2 onions, chopped
Mushrooms

In crockpot put roast, mushroom soup, wine and Ranch dressing. Cook until tender, 6 to 8 hours on low. Add onions and mushrooms 30 minutes before serving. Serve with rice.

POT ROAST & GRAVY

1 beef roast
1½ c. water
1 can golden mushroom soup

3 T. flour
1 tsp. garlic seasoning

Combine all ingredients in a crockpot. Simmer on low 8 hours or until tender.

CROCK-98

BEEF & MUSHROOMS

Rump roast or lean beef
Flour
Cooking oil
1 can mushroom soup
1 c. beef broth
1 can mushrooms

1 c. milk
1 c. water
Garlic powder
Salt & pepper
Italian seasoning

Cut beef into chunks. Roll in flour and brown in small amount of oil. Put all ingredients into crockpot and cook on low 10 to 12 hours. Serve over noodles or rice.

POSOLE (An Indian Recipe)

1 lb. beef roast
Salt & pepper
1 lb. pinto beans, cooked &
  seasoned

2½ c. drained hominy
1 sm. can chopped green chilies

Cook meat with salt and pepper in pressure cooker. Cut into small bite-sized pieces. Place meat and other ingredients in crockpot and simmer on low until flavorful and rather thick.

SLOW COOKER ROAST ITALIAN

3 to 3½-lb. boneless chuck
  roast
2 T. vegetable oil
1 med. onion, sliced
1 green pepper, sliced

1 (4-oz.) can mushrooms,
  drained
¼ c. Parmesan cheese
2 c. Italian dressing (bottled or
  homemade)

Brown roast well on both sides in oil. Place onion, green pepper and mushrooms in crockpot. Place meat on top. Add cheese and dressing; cover and cook on low setting 9 to 10 hours. Serve with noodles, if desired.

CROCK-98

BOURBON 'N BEEF ROAST (EASY)

4 potatoes, pared & quartered
2 carrots, pared & cut into 3-in.
  pieces
2 stalks celery, cut up
4 to 5-lb. rolled roast

1 bay leaf
½ tsp. basil
4 oz. bourbon
¼ c. water

Put all ingredients in crockpot. Cover and cook on low 10 to 12 hours or on high 5 to 6 hours.

BELGIAN BEEF

3 to 5-lb. pot roast, sprinkled
  with salt & pepper
1-2 lg. onions, thickly sliced
4 cloves garlic, mashed
1 (12-oz.) can beer
1 beef bouillon cube
2 T. brown sugar

2 tsp. salt (if desired)
1 T. parsley
½ tsp. thyme
1 bay leaf, crumbled
Thickening (add after cooking):
2 T. cornstarch
3 T. wine vinegar

Place roast in crockpot. Cover with onions. Mix remaining ingredients and pour over meat. Cook on low all day. When done, drain sauce into another pan; skim off fat. Thicken sauce with mixture of cornstarch and vinegar. Meat will fall into chunks easily. Pour sauce back over it and keep warm in crockpot until serving. Serve with hot, buttered noodles or tiny new potatoes.

BEER BRAISED BEEF

4 lbs. beef chuck, cut in 2-in. pieces
½ c. flour
2 T. salt
2 tsp. paprika
1 tsp. pepper
10-12 whole sm. onions, peeled
4 strips bacon, cut in sm. pieces
1 lb. fresh mushrooms, sliced (or two 8-oz. cans)
1 (12-oz.) can beer
1 tsp. sugar
1 T. vinegar
2 tsp. dried thyme, crushed
1 bay leaf

Thoroughly coat beef cubes with flour, salt, paprika and pepper in large bowl or paper sack. Place onions, bacon and half of sliced mushrooms in crockpot. Add floured beef cubes and remaining half of mushrooms. Mix beer with sugar, vinegar, thyme and bay leaf. Pour into crockpot. Cover and cook on low for 8 to 10 hours. Serve over noodles or rice.
Note: May be thickened, if desired. Make a smooth paste of 3 tablespoons flour mixed with ½ cup water. Pour into beef mixture. Turn to high and allow to come to a simmer, about 10 minutes.

BOEUF BOURGUIGNONNE

3 lbs. beef rump round, cut in 1½-in. cubes
3 T. butter
1 lg. onion, sliced
1 lg. garlic clove, chopped
½ c. all-purpose flour
1 c. dry red wine
1 (10½-oz.) can beef broth
2 T. tomato paste
1 tsp. thyme, crushed
1 bay leaf
½ lb. sm. white onions, peeled
½ lb. fresh mushrooms
Salt
Pepper

Brown beef cubes in hot butter. Remove cubes to crockpot. In drippings, cook onion and garlic 5 minutes. Sprinkle with flour. Slowly stir in wine, beef broth and tomato paste. Cook until sauce bubbles and thickens. Add thyme, bay leaf, white onions and mushrooms. Pour over beef. Season with salt and pepper. Cook on low 9 to 12 hours or high 5 to 6 hours. Remove bay leaf.

BEEF A LA MODE

1½ tsp. salt
1 tsp. thyme
1 tsp. pepper
1 carrot, chopped
1 celery stalk, chopped
1 onion, chopped
2 garlic cloves, minced

1 c. dry red wine
4 lb. beef roast
1 T. butter
2 T. beef bouillon
¼ c. tomato sauce
Parsley

Make marinade by combining salt, thyme, pepper, carrot, celery, onion, garlic and red wine. Place roast in marinade, and cover and chill 1 day. Remove from marinade and pat dry with paper towel. Brown roast in butter. Place in crockpot. Add marinade, beef bouillon and tomato sauce. Cover and cook on low 8 hours or until meat is tender. Transfer meat to carving board. Pour juices into saucepan. Boil until reduced to 2 cups. Serve in a sauce bowl. Garnish with parsley.

SAUERBRATEN

2 c. dry white wine
2 c. white vinegar
2 c. water
2 lg. onions, sliced
2 lg. carrots, sliced
6 peppercorns
4 bay leaves

6 whole cloves
1 tsp. mustard seed
1 T. dried parsley flakes
2 tsp. salt
5-lb. bottom round or rump
  roast

Combine all of the above ingredients except roast; heat to boil. Simmer for 15 minutes; cool. Pour over meat and refrigerate. Marinate for 3 to 4 days, turning once a day.

4 T. all-purpose flour
1 tsp. salt
¼ tsp. pepper

2 T. oil
2 T. sugar
⅓ c. gingersnap crumbs

Remove meat from marinade; discard vegetables; reserve marinade. Mix 2 tablespoons flour, salt and pepper. Coat towel-dried meat. Brown in oil. Place in crockpot. Add 1½ cups strained marinade. Cover; cook on low 8 hours. Combine sugar, remaining 2 tablespoons of flour and gingersnap crumbs. Add to crockpot and stir well. Cover. Turn crockpot to high; cook 30 minutes. Serve with potato pancakes.

POT AU FEU

2 lbs. boneless rump or chuck
  pot roast, cut into 6 pieces
1 lb. pork tenderloin or well-
  trimmed pork chops
2-3 chicken breasts or thighs,
  halved
1/2 lb. Polish sausage, cut in
  serving pieces
3 carrots, pared & cut in 3-in.
  pieces
2 onions, peeled, halved & stuck
  with whole cloves

2 parsnips, pared (opt.)
2 stalks celery, cut in 2-in.
  pieces
1 bay leaf
6 peppercorns
1/2 tsp. thyme
4 garlic cloves, minced
1 (10-oz.) can beef bouillon
Salt to taste

Alternate pieces of meat in crockpot with sausage on top. Add vegetables on sides to fill up. Wrap bay leaf, peppercorns, thyme and garlic in cheesecloth and put in the approximate center. Pour in bouillon. Cover and cook on low 12 to 18 hours. Serve with cooked carrots, onions, parsnips and celery.

BEEF FAJITAS (EASY)

1 1/2 lbs. beef flank steak
1 onion, sliced
1 green pepper in strips
1 red pepper in strips
1 jalapeño pepper, chopped
1 tsp. chili powder

1 tsp. cumin
1 T. cilantro
1 tsp. coriander
1/4 tsp. salt
1 (8-oz.) can tomatoes

Cut flank steak into 6 portions. Put all ingredients in crockpot. Cover and cook on low 8 hours or on high 4 1/2 hours. Remove meat (when cooked completely) and shred. Return to crockpot and stir.

SMOKED ROAST SANDWICH

5 to 6-lb. roast
1/4 c. smoke flavor
1/2 tsp. onion salt

1/2 tsp. garlic salt
1/2 tsp. celery salt

Place roast on foil with smoke flavoring. Sprinkle with salts. Wrap tightly. Cook on low 8 to 12 hours in crockpot. Slice and serve on buns or with potatoes.

PIT BARBECUE BEEF SANDWICH

3 to 5-lb. roast
½ c. salt
⅓ c. flour
1 T. pepper
¾ tsp. garlic salt

¾ tsp. turmeric
1½ tsp. chili powder
1 T. hickory smoke
1 bay leaf

Mix all ingredients together and rub generously over roast. Wrap in foil. Place in crockpot and cook on high 1 to 2 hours, then turn to low to finish cooking. Cooking time depends on size of roast. Slice and serve on buns.

EASY CROCKPOT BAR-B-Q SANDWICH

5-6 lbs. beef roast
1 qt. dill pickles & juice (whole or sliced)

2 bottles chili sauce

Put roast in crockpot and add pickles and chili sauce. Leave on high until juices start to boil, then turn on low. Cook about 15 hours. Mash the pickles up with a fork and leave in crockpot. The beef will shred easily with a fork. Serve on buns.

SLOW-SIMMERED BARBECUE SANDWICH

3-lb. beef brisket
½ c. water
3 T. vinegar
2 T. Worcestershire sauce
1 tsp. ground cumin

3 c. barbecue sauce
12-16 kaiser rolls or hamburger
  buns
Dill pickles
Red onion slices

Trim fat off beef and cut to fit into crockpot. Add water, vinegar, Worcestershire sauce and cumin. Cover and cook on low 10 to 12 hours or on high 4 to 5 hours. About 1 hour before serving, remove meat. Drain and shred. Place shredded meat back in crockpot. Stir in barbecue sauce and cook on high 30 to 45 minutes. Serve on buns with pickles and red onion slices.

ZESTY BBQ BEEF SANDWICH

¾ c. cola (not diet)
½ tsp. dry mustard
½ tsp. chili powder
¼ c. Worcestershire sauce
1 T. vinegar
2 cloves garlic, minced
1 tsp. beef bouillon

1½ lbs. boneless beef chuck
  roast
2 med. onions, chopped
½ c. ketchup
2 T. butter
¼ c. barbecue sauce
Brown sugar

Mix together cola, dry mustard, chili powder, Worcestershire sauce, vinegar, garlic and beef bouillon to make cooking liquid. Trim fat from meat; place in crockpot and cover with onions. Pour half of the cooking liquid over all. Cook 10 to 12 hours at low or 5 to 6 hours at high. Next, heat in small pan remaining liquid, ketchup, butter and barbecue sauce. Add brown sugar to sweeten if needed. When meat is done, discard onions and cooking liquid. Shred meat and pour sauce over the meat; mix well.

BARBECUED BEEF IN HOMEMADE SAUCE

1 (5-lb.) chuck beef roast or
  brisket
1 T. liquid smoke
½ tsp. garlic powder
½ tsp. onion powder

2 tsp. celery seed
Salt to taste
2 tsp. Worcestershire sauce
2 T. soy sauce

Mix all ingredients together except meat. Place meat in crockpot and pour liquid over it. Cook on low 8 to 10 hours. During the last hour, add sauce.

Sauce:

¼ c. water
1 c. tomato sauce
¼ c. onion, chopped
1 T. liquid smoke
½ tsp. celery seed

1 T. vinegar
⅓-½ c. brown sugar
1 tsp. mustard
1 T. Worcestershire sauce

Mix together and simmer in a saucepan 10 minutes. Cover meat with sauce. Shred meat and serve.

FRENCH DIP SANDWICH

1 lean beef roast	1 pkg. French au jus sauce mix
1 can beef consomme	1 pkg. Italian dressing mix
1 can water	

Place all ingredients in crockpot. Cook all day on low. Meat should come apart easily when done. Serve on hoagie buns or French sour dough buns and dip in juice.

ITALIAN BEEF SANDWICH (EASY)

4 to 5-lb. roast	1 can beef consomme
1 can onion soup	2 T. Italian seasoning

Put roast in crockpot. Add undiluted soup, consomme and seasoning. Cook 4 to 5 hours on high or 8 to 10 hours on low. Shred meat when done. Serve on Italian rolls. May be frozen and reheated on stove top.

STEAKS

COUNTRY-FRIED STEAK

Salt & pepper	Oil
2 lbs. cubed steak	Water
Flour	

Salt and pepper steak to taste; coat with flour. Heat a little oil in frying pan. Brown steak on both sides. Stand in crockpot with flat sides toward side of pot. Repeat this as many times as needed for all pieces. Make gravy by browning about 4 tablespoons flour and salt and pepper to taste in pan drippings. Add enough water to make thin gravy. Pour over steak and cook on low about 4 hours.

CROCK-98

MUSHROOM STEAK

2½ lbs. round steak, cut up
2 T. oil
2 cans cream of mushroom
  soup

½ soup can water

Brown meat in hot oil in skillet. Remove meat to crockpot. Add soup and water. Cover and cook on low 6 hours or until very tender. Serve over mashed potatoes or rice.

COUNTRY-STYLE STEAK

1 lb. cubed steak
Flour
2 T. oil

¼ c. onion, chopped
1 can cream of mushroom soup
1 c. water

Coat steak with flour and brown in skillet in oil. Place in crockpot. Sprinkle onion over steak. Combine soup and water. Stir into pan drippings. Bring to a boil. Pour over steak. Cook on low 4 hours or until steak is tender.

BEER STEAK

3 lbs. round steak, cut in
  serving size pieces
⅓ c. flour

1 can beer
1 env. dry onion soup mix
1 env. brown gravy mix

In plastic bag shake meat and flour. Put in crockpot, then add beer, soup mix and gravy mix. Cook on low 8 hours.

BEEF BURGUNDY (EASY)

2 cans cream of mushroom
  soup
2 lbs. sirloin, cut in strips

1 (6 to 8-oz.) can mushrooms
½ c. Burgundy (or sherry)
1 pkg. dry onion soup mix

Mix all ingredients together. Bake, covered, in crockpot 12 to 14 hours on low or 6 to 8 hours on high. Serve over noodles.

ROUND STEAK & RICH GRAVY

2-2½ lbs. round steak
1 pkg. dry onion soup mix
¼ c. water

1 can condensed cream of
  mushroom soup

Cut steak into 5 to 6 serving pieces. Place in crockpot. Add dry onion soup mix, water and condensed mushroom soup. Cover and cook on low 6 to 8 hours. Excellent served over mashed potatoes.

COUNTRY STEAK AND ONION GRAVY

2-lbs. round steak, cut in
  serving pieces
Flour
½ c. vegetable oil

1 tsp. salt
¼ tsp. pepper
2 cans cream of onion soup
1 c. water

Trim all fat from steak. Roll in flour and brown in oil in skillet. Add salt and pepper. When browned put in crockpot, then add cream of onion soup and water. Let cook on low 3 to 4 hours. Serve with mashed or baked potatoes.

CROCKPOT STROGANOFF

1 env. dry onion soup mix
1 can cream of celery soup
1 can cream of mushroom soup

1½ lbs. round steak, cubed
1 can mushrooms
½ c. sour cream

Mix soup mix, soups and steak. Cook in crockpot 4 hours or more on high. Stir in mushrooms and sour cream about 10 minutes before serving. Serve over cooked noodles or rice. (Can be cooked on low for 8 hours or more.)

CROCK-98

EASY CUBED STEAK

Salt
Pepper
Flour
2 lbs. round or cubed steak
Cooking oil
1 can cream of golden
  mushroom soup

1 can cream of celery soup
1 (15-oz.) can tomato sauce
1 T. minced onion
1 sm. can mushrooms, drained

Salt, pepper and flour steak. Brown in oil in skillet. Mix both cans of soup, tomato sauce, onion and mushrooms. Alternate layers of sauce and steak in crockpot. Cook on low about 6 hours or on high about 3 hours.

STEAK IN CROCKPOT

2 lbs. round steak
Flour
Salt
Dry mustard
Paprika
1/2 c. onion, chopped

1/4 c. oil
3 T. oleo
3/4 c. water
3 T. soy sauce
3 T. brown sugar
3/4-1 c. sour cream

Dredge steak in flour, salt, mustard and paprika. Place in crockpot. Mix remaining ingredients together and pour over meat. Cook 6 to 8 hours on low.

SPICY CROCKPOT STEAK

Top round steak or top sirloin
3 T. oil
3 T. water
Salt & pepper
1 T. vinegar
2 tsp. garlic powder

1 1/2 T. crushed basil
1 T. steak sauce
Bacon
1 lg. onion, sliced
1 lg. green pepper, sliced

Tenderize steak with a fork. Cut in strips 3 to 4 inches wide. Sauté in oil until brown. Add water; season with salt and pepper, vinegar, garlic powder, basil and steak sauce. Cook another minute or two, then turn off heat and let marinate for 20 minutes. Lay each strip on a strip of bacon. Roll and secure with a toothpick. Place in crockpot and pour juice over. Lay onion and green pepper on top of steaks. Add more salt and pepper. Cook on low all day. Serve over rice.

CROCK-98

BEEF & VEGETABLES IN RED WINE SAUCE

1½ lbs. boneless beef bottom round steak, cut into 1-in. cubes
1 T. cooking oil
2 med. carrots, cut into ½-in. pieces
2 stalks celery, cut into ½-in. pieces
1 c. fresh mushrooms, quartered
½ c. green onions, sliced
3 T. quick-cooking tapioca
1 (14½-oz.) can Italian-style stewed tomatoes
1 c. beef broth
½ c. dry red wine, white wine or beef broth
1 tsp. dried Italian seasoning, crushed
½ tsp. salt
¼ tsp. pepper
1 bay leaf
3 c. hot, cooked noodles

In a large skillet brown beef, one-half at a time, in hot oil; drain off fat. Transfer beef to a 3½ or 4-quart crockpot. Add carrots, celery, mushrooms and green onions. Sprinkle with tapioca. Combine un-drained tomatoes, beef broth, wine or broth, Italian seasoning, salt, pepper and bay leaf. Pour over vegetables and meat. Cover; cook on low 8 to 10 hours or on high 4 to 5 hours. Discard bay leaf. Serve over hot, cooked noodles.

POKEY POT PEPPER STEAK

1½-2 lbs. beef round steak
2 T. cooking oil
¼ c. soy sauce
1 c. onion, chopped or minced onion
Garlic to taste
1 tsp. sugar
½ tsp. salt
¼ tsp. pepper
¼ tsp. ground ginger
4 tomatoes, cut into eighths (or 1 can tomatoes)
2 green peppers, cut into strips
1 T. cornstarch
½ c. cold water
Cooked noodles, rice or orzo pasta

Cut beef into 3 x 1-inch strips; brown in skillet with oil. Transfer to crockpot. Combine soy sauce, onion, garlic, sugar, salt, pepper and ginger; pour over beef. Cover and cook on low 5 to 6 hours or until meat is tender. Add tomatoes and peppers; cook on low 1 hour longer. Combine cornstarch and water to make a paste; stir into liquid in the crockpot and cook on high until thickened. Serve over noodles, rice or orzo pasta.

CROCK-98

GOURMET SMOTHERED PEPPER STEAK

1½ lbs. round steak, cut in
  strips
⅓ c. flour
1 tsp. salt
½ tsp. pepper
1 lg. onion, sliced

1-2 green peppers, sliced
1 (1-lb.) can tomatoes
1 (4-oz.) can mushrooms,
  drained
3 T. soy sauce

Put steak strips, flour, salt and pepper in crockpot. Stir well to coat steaks. Add all remaining ingredients. Cover and cook on high 1 hour, then turn to low for 8 hours (or high for 5 hours). Serve over rice.

SWEET & SOUR BEEF & VEGGIES

2 round or chuck steaks, cut in
  1-in. cubes
2 T. vegetable oil
2 (8-oz.) cans tomato sauce
¼ c. sugar
½ c. vinegar
2 c. carrots, sliced 1 in. thick

1 lg. green pepper, cut in 1-in.
  squares
2 tsp. chili powder
2 tsp. paprika
1 tsp. salt
½ c. light molasses
2 sm. white onions, peeled

Brown meat in hot oil in skillet. Transfer to crockpot. Add remaining ingredients; mix well. Cook 6 to 7 hours on low or 4 hours on high. Serve with salad, pasta or rice and French bread.

SWISS STEAK MOZZARELLA

2 lbs. beef round steak, cut ½
  in. thick
3 T. flour
¼ c. butter
1 (1-lb.) can tomatoes
¾ tsp. salt

¼ tsp. basil
½ c. green pepper, chopped
½ c. onion, chopped
1½ c. mozzarella cheese,
  shredded

Dredge steak in flour. Melt butter in skillet. Brown beef slowly on both sides. Transfer meat to crockpot. Add tomatoes, salt and basil. Top with peppers and onions. Cook on low until meat is tender. Top with cheese.

CROCK-98

SAUCY STEAK

1 lb. round steak, cut into
  serving pieces
¼ c. flour
1 T. vegetable oil
1 lg. onion, chopped
Water
1 (16-oz.) can whole potatoes,
  drained (reserve liquid)
¼ c. ketchup

1 T. Worcestershire sauce
2 tsp. bell pepper flakes
1 tsp. instant beef bouillon
1 tsp. salt
½ tsp. dried marjoram leaves
¼ tsp. pepper
1 can cut green or Italian green
  beans

Coat meat with flour; pound into meat. Brown meat in oil. Push to side. Cook onion in oil until tender; drain. Add enough water to potato liquid to measure 1 cup. Mix potato liquid, ketchup, Worcestershire sauce, pepper flakes, bouillon, salt, marjoram and pepper. Place beef and onion in crockpot and cover with liquid, potatoes and beans. Cook on low for 8 to 10 hours.

SMOTHERED STEAK

1½ lbs. round steak, cubed
⅓ c. flour
¼ c. oil
Salt & pepper
1 onion, sliced & ringed
2 green peppers, chopped
2 c. celery, diced

1 (1-lb.) can whole tomatoes
1 (4-oz.) jar mushrooms, sliced
1 (10-oz.) box frozen French-
  style green beans
2 T. molasses
4 T. soy sauce
½ tsp. salt

Dredge meat in flour and brown in oil. Salt and pepper meat. Place meat in crockpot, then layer remaining ingredients on top of the meat in the order listed. Cook on low 6 to 8 hours or until done. Serve over rice.

STUFFED FLANK STEAK

1½ c. packaged bread stuffing
2 T. melted butter
2 T. water
2 T. grated Parmesan cheese

1 to 1½-lb. flank steak, scored
2 T. salad oil
1 pkg. brown gravy mix

Combine bread stuffing with butter, water and cheese. Spread over flank steak; roll up like jellyroll. Fasten with skewers. Pour oil in crockpot. Roll steak in oil, coating all sides. Prepare gravy as directed and pour over meat. Cover and cook on low 8 to 10 hours.

MEXICAN BEEF

2-2½ lbs. boneless round steak, ½ in. thick
1 clove garlic, chopped or ½ tsp. garlic powder
¼ tsp. pepper
½ tsp. salt
1 T. chili powder

1 T. prepared mustard
1 onion, chopped
1 beef bouillon cube
1 can tomatoes, cut up
1 (16-oz.) can kidney beans, drained

Rub meat with seasonings and mustard. Place in crockpot. Cover with onion, bouillon cube and tomatoes. Cover and cook on low 6 to 8 hours. Turn to high; add beans and cook, covered, for 30 minutes. Serve on bed of rice or noodles.

TERIYAKI STEAK (EASY)

2-2½ lbs. chuck steak
1 tsp. ground ginger
1 T. sugar

2 T. oil
½ c. soy sauce
1 clove garlic, crushed

Cut meat into ⅛-inch slices. Combine remaining ingredients in a small bowl. Place meat in crockpot. Pour sauce over. Cover and cook on low 5 to 6 hours. Serve with rice.

CHINESE PEPPER STEAK

1 to 1½-lb. round steak
2 T. oil
1 clove garlic, minced
½ tsp. salt
¼ tsp. pepper
¼ c. soy sauce
1 tsp. sugar
1 c. fresh or canned bean sprouts, drained

1 c. canned tomatoes, cut up
2 green peppers, seeded & cut into strips
1 T. cornstarch
2 T. cold water
4 green onions, sliced

Slice steak into narrow strips. In skillet brown steak in oil. Combine with garlic, salt, pepper, soy sauce and sugar in crockpot. Cook on low 6 to 8 hours. Turn control to high. Add bean sprouts, tomatoes and green peppers. Dissolve cornstarch in water; stir into pot. Cover and cook 15 to 20 minutes or until thickened. Sprinkle with onions.

CROCK-98

CHINESE BEEF & SNOW PEAS

1 to 1½-lb. flank steak
1 (10½-oz.) can condensed beef
  consomme
¼ c. soy sauce
¼ tsp. ground ginger
1 bunch green onions, sliced
2 T. cornstarch
2 T. cold water
1 (7-oz.) pkg. frozen Chinese
  snow peas, partially thawed

Thinly slice flank steak diagonally across the grain. Combine strips in crockpot with consomme, soy sauce, ginger and onions. Cover and cook on low for 5 to 7 hours. Turn control to high. Stir in cornstarch that has been dissolved in the cold water. Cook on high 10 to 15 minutes or until thickened. Drop in pea pods the last 5 minutes. Serve over hot rice.

CHINESE BROCCOLI BEEF

1 lb. round steak
1 (10-oz.) can beef consomme
¼ c. soy sauce
1 tsp. onion powder
2 T. cornstarch
2 T. cold water
1 bunch fresh broccoli, cut in
  pieces
Rice, cooked

Thinly slice round steak in strips. In crockpot combine steak, consomme, soy sauce and onion powder. Cover and cook on low 6 to 7 hours. Turn on high and stir in cornstarch dissolved in cold water. Cook on high for 10 to 15 minutes or until thick. Add broccoli and cook 5 minutes more. Serve over cooked rice.

STEW MEAT OR TIPS

BEEF TIPS & NOODLES

1½ lbs. stew meat
Salt, pepper & garlic salt to
  taste
4 c. water
2 pkgs. dry onion soup mix
1 pkg. egg noodles

Put stew meat in crockpot. Add salt, pepper and garlic salt. Pour water over meat. Add onion soup and let cook on low all day or on high 6 hours. Cook noodles according to package directions. Drain; put in crockpot and cook 20 minutes longer. Serve.

CROCK-98

BEEF TIPS & RICE

1 pkg. stew beef or beef steak,
  cut into cubes
1 can golden mushroom soup

Water
1 c. prepared rice

Put beef in crockpot and cover with soup. A little water may be added to make a thick soup. Cook on low approximately 8 hours. Serve over rice.

CREAMY BEEF TIPS EASY

2 pkgs. stew meat
1 pkg. dry onion soup mix
2 cans undiluted mushroom
  soup

2 c. ginger ale or 1 c. apple
  juice

Cut off fat from stew meat and place in crockpot. Add remaining ingredients. Simmer on low all day. Serve over rice or egg noodles.

MEXICAN BEEF TIPS

3 lbs. beef stew meat
1 (10-oz.) can cream of celery
  soup
1 (4-oz.) can chopped green
  chilies

Garlic (opt.)
Flour tortillas
Cheddar or Jack cheese,
  shredded

Combine all ingredients in crockpot; stir well to coat meat. Cook on high 6 to 8 hours. It should fall apart when done. Use a potato masher to blend liquid and separate meat. Put meat mixture into a tortilla with grated cheddar or Jack cheese. Serve hot. Can be used for burritos, soft tacos, tostadas, bean dip or served over rice.

SHERRIED BEEF EASY

2 c. cream of mushroom soup
3/4 c. cooking sherry
1 pkg. dry onion soup mix

2-3 lbs. stew meat
1 lb. fresh mushrooms, sliced

In crockpot mix soup, sherry and onion soup mix. Put in beef and sliced mushrooms and mix together. Cook on low 8 hours. Serve over cooked noodles.

CROCK-98

DELUXE BEEF CUBES

1½ lbs. chuck cubes
1 pkg. dry onion mushroom
  soup mix
3 beef bouillon cubes, dissolved
  in 1½ c. boiling water
1 sm. green pepper, sliced
¾ tsp. garlic powder

1 tsp. seasoned salt
½ tsp. coarse ground pepper
½ tsp. salt
Flour
1 (10 to 16-oz.) pkg. med.
  noodles, cooked

Put all ingredients except flour and noodles in crockpot. Cook on low 8 to 10 hours. Thicken juices with flour and serve over cooked noodles.

BEEF & ONIONS

3 lbs. beef, cubed
1 env. dry onion soup mix
¼ c. burgundy wine
Seasoned salt

Pepper
2 med. onions, sliced
Margarine
1 can cream of mushroom soup

Place beef, soup mix, wine, seasoned salt, pepper and 1 onion in crockpot and cook on low all day; drain, keeping liquid. Sauté second onion in the margarine until browned. Add soup and then add mixture to drained meat in crockpot. Serve over rice or noodles.

HEARTY BEEF TIPS

½ c. flour
1 tsp. salt
⅛ tsp. pepper
4 lbs. beef or sirloin tips, cubed
½ c. green onion, chopped
2 (4-oz.) cans sliced mushrooms
1 (10½-oz.) can condensed beef
  broth

1 tsp. Worcestershire sauce
2 tsp. tomato paste or ketchup
¼ c. water
3 T. flour
Buttered noodles

Combine ½ cup flour with salt and pepper; toss with beef cubes to coat. Place in crockpot. Add onions and mushrooms. Combine beef broth, Worcestershire sauce and tomato paste. Pour over beef and vegetables; stir well. Cook on low 7 to 12 hours. One hour before serving, turn to high. Make a smooth paste with water and 3 tablespoons flour. Stir in crockpot; mix well. Cover and cook until thickened. Serve over hot buttered noodles.

CROCKPOT HASH

3 c. cooked beef, cubed
1 c. onions, chopped
24 oz. frozen hash brown
  potatoes, loosened and
  defrosted

1 env. brown gravy mix
1 c. water
¼ c. margarine
1 tsp. salt
½ tsp. pepper

Put beef and onion in crockpot. Stir in hash browns. Mix gravy and water. Add to crockpot. Dot with margarine. Add salt and pepper. Cook 7 to 9 hours on low.

TERIYAKI SHREDDED BEEF (EASY)

2 lbs. stewing beef
¼ c. onion, diced
¾ c. celery, diced
½-1 c. teriyaki sauce

Dash of garlic powder
Dash of lemon pepper
½ c. water

Put all ingredients in a crockpot. Cook on low approximately 6 hours, stirring occasionally. When cooked thoroughly, shred meat with 2 forks. Great with rolls for sandwiches. Can be frozen and reheated later.

BEEF BURGUNDY

6 strips bacon, cut in ½-in.
  pieces
2-3 lbs. beef, cut in chunks
1 lg. carrot, pared
1 med. onion, sliced
1½ tsp. salt
⅛ tsp. pepper
3 T. flour

1 (10-oz.) can beef broth
1 T. tomato paste
½-1 tsp. thyme
1½ c. burgundy wine
1 lb. fresh mushrooms, sliced
½ lb. white onions, peeled
Cooked noodles

Cook bacon until crisp. Brown beef in grease. Place in crockpot. Sauté carrot and onion. Season with salt and pepper. Stir in flour. Add broth; mix well and add tomato paste, thyme and wine to crockpot. Cover and cook on low 6 to 8 hours. Turn control to high. Add mushrooms and onions. Cook 15 minutes. Serve over cooked noodles.

EASY BEEF STROGANOFF

1-2 lbs. stew beef
1 can beef consomme
1 can cream of mushroom soup

1 sm. jar sliced mushrooms
Salt & pepper
1 pkg. egg noodles

Combine all ingredients except noodles and salt and pepper in crockpot; stir well. Cook on low 6 to 8 hours. Salt and pepper to taste. Cook egg noodles as directed. Serve over noodles.

CROCKPOT BEEF STROGANOFF

3 lbs. stew beef
Flour
2 T. oil
2 onions, chopped fine
½ c. flour
2 (10½-oz.) cans tomato soup
2 (10½-oz.) cans beef
  consomme
½ c. red wine

8 oz. fresh mushrooms (or
  drained, canned mushrooms)
4 tsp. Worcestershire sauce
1 c. sour cream
2 tsp. paprika
Salt & pepper to taste

Cut stew beef in bite-sized pieces. Flour and brown meat in skillet in hot oil. This must be done in 3 batches, 1 pound at a time. On the last pound of meat, add onions and sauté. Place meat in crockpot. Pour ¼ cup of flour over meat; stir well. Add soup, consomme, wine, mushrooms and Worcestershire sauce; cook at least 5 hours on low. After meat is tender, add sour cream and paprika. Thicken by taking ½ cup sauce and adding remaining flour. Return to pot; stir. Simmer until thickened. Serve over long-grain rice or buttered noodles.

CROCK-98

HUNGARIAN GOULASH

2 lbs. beef stew meat, cut into
  1-in. cubes
1 lg. onion, sliced
1 clove garlic, minced
½ c. ketchup
2 T. Worcestershire sauce
1 T. brown sugar

1 tsp. salt
2 tsp. paprika
½ tsp. dry mustard
1 c. water
¼ c. flour
Cold water

Place meat in crockpot. Cover with sliced onion. Combine garlic, ketchup, Worcestershire sauce, sugar, salt, paprika and mustard. Stir in 1 cup water. Pour over meat. Cover and cook on low 9 to 10 hours. Turn on high. Dissolve flour in small amount of cold water; stir into meat mixture. Cook on high 10 to 15 minutes or until slightly thickened. Serve goulash over noodles or rice.

HAMBURGER

CROCKPOT MEAT LOAF

1 egg, beaten
¼ c. milk
1½ tsp. salt
1 tsp. onion flakes

2 slices bread, crumbled
1½ lbs. ground beef
Ketchup (sm. amount)

Mix egg, milk, salt, onion and bread crumbs. Combine with ground beef. Shape into loaf and place in crockpot. Top with ketchup. Cover, set on low and cook for 8 to 9 hours.

DELUXE MEAT LOAF

2 lbs. ground beef
1 pkg. meat loaf seasoning
4 med. potatoes
4 carrots
Salt
Pepper
1 can cream of mushroom soup
1 can spinach

Red onion, diced
Bacon bits
½ lb. Swiss cheese
⅔ c. ketchup
1 T. mustard
1 tsp. Worcestershire sauce
2 T. brown sugar

Mix ground beef with meat loaf seasoning as directed on package. Pare and slice potatoes and carrots. Put in bottom of crockpot and season with salt and pepper. Add can of mushroom soup and stir well so vegetables are coated. Put ½ of meat mixture on top of vegetables. Layer with spinach and red onion; sprinkle with bacon bits and Swiss cheese. Add remaining meat loaf mixture and pat down well. Top with ketchup, mustard, Worcestershire sauce and brown sugar (all mixed well). Cook on high at least 3 hours or on low most of the day or until vegetables are tender.

MEXICAN MEAT LOAF

2 lbs. ground beef
1 c. corn chips, coarsely
   crushed
⅓ c. taco sauce

1 egg, lightly beaten
2 T. taco seasoning mix
½ c. cheddar or Monterey Jack
   cheese, grated

Mix all ingredients together and shape into a loaf. Place in crockpot; cover and cook on low 8 hours.

MOCK STEAK

3 lbs. ground beef
1 c. water
1 c. crackers, finely crushed
Flour
Salt & pepper to taste

1 can cream of celery soup
1 can cream of mushroom soup
1 can cream of chicken soup
Onion, sliced

Mix ground beef, water and crackers; press out thin onto a 15½ x 10½ x 1-inch sheet pan. Cut in squares. Freeze. Roll in flour, salt and pepper, and fry until brown. Put meat in crockpot and pour soups over. Onion slices may be added. Cover. Cook for 4 to 5 hours on low.

CROCK-98

ITALIAN BEEF & POTATO CASSEROLE

1 lb. ground beef
1 (16-oz.) can tomatoes
1/2 c. water
1/2 tsp. salt
1/2 tsp. oregano

1/8 tsp. garlic powder
1 (5 1/2-oz.) pkg. scalloped
  potatoes and sauce mix
1 c. mozzarella cheese cubes
1/4 c. Parmesan cheese

Brown and drain ground beef. Mix all ingredients except cheeses in crockpot. Cover and cook on low 4 to 5 hours. Turn to high and stir in cheese cubes. Sprinkle with Parmesan cheese. Cook 10 to 15 minutes.

HAMBURGER-VEGETABLE CROCKPOT MEAL

1 lb. ground beef
1 med. onion, chopped
1 clove of garlic, chopped
2 c. potatoes, sliced
1 c. carrots, sliced

1 can sweet peas, drained
1 can tomato soup
1 c. water
1 T. steak sauce

Brown ground beef with onion and garlic; drain. In crockpot layer potatoes, carrots, peas and ground beef in that order. Mix tomato soup, water and steak sauce. Pour over ingredients in crockpot. Cook on low 8 hours or high 4 hours.

ITALIAN MEATBALLS

1 1/2-2 lbs. ground beef
2 eggs
1 1/4 c. Italian bread crumbs
1 pkg. dry onion soup mix
1/4 c. onion flakes

1 bottle barbecue sauce
1 (20-oz.) can chunky
  pineapple & juice
1 can black pitted olives,
  drained

Mix together ground beef, eggs, bread crumbs, soup mix and onion flakes; roll into balls; freeze. Broil frozen meatballs until brown on both sides. Place meatballs in crockpot. Add barbecue sauce, pineapple, pineapple juice and olives. Cook on low about 4 hours.

CROCK-98

HEARTY BEEF POT PIE

2 lbs. beef round steak, cut into
  1-in. cubes
3 T. flour
1 tsp. salt
⅛ tsp. pepper
2 med. carrots, pared & sliced
3 med. potatoes, pared & sliced
1 lg. onion, thinly sliced
1 (16-oz.) can whole tomatoes
Biscuit Topping

Place steak cubes in crockpot. Combine flour, salt and pepper; toss with steak to coat thoroughly. Stir in remaining ingredients except Biscuit Topping; mix thoroughly. Cover and cook on low 8 to 10 hours or on high 4 to 5 hours. One hour before serving, remove meat and vegetables from crockpot and pour into shallow 2½-quart baking dish. Preheat oven to 425°. Cover meat mixture with Biscuit Topping. Bake for 20 to 25 minutes.

Biscuit Topping:

2 c. flour
1 tsp. salt
3 tsp. baking powder
¼ c. shortening
¾ c. milk

Mix dry ingredients. Cut in shortening until mixture resembles coarse cornmeal. Add milk all at one time; stir well. Pat out on floured board. Roll out to cover baking dish.

CALIFORNIA PILAF (EASY)

2 lbs. ground beef
2½ c. water
2 (8-oz.) cans tomato sauce
1 green pepper, chopped
2 sm. garlic cloves, minced
  (opt.)
1 sm. onion, chopped
2½ tsp. salt
¼ tsp. pepper
⅔ c. ripe olives, sliced
1⅓ c. raw rice (long grain)

Brown ground beef in skillet; drain off fat. Place ground beef and all remaining ingredients in crockpot; stir well. Cover and cook on low 5 to 6 hours or on high 3 hours.

TEXAS HASH

2 lbs. ground beef	1½ tsp. chili powder
2 med. onions, chopped	2½ tsp. salt
2 green peppers, chopped	2 tsp. Worcestershire sauce
2 (1-lb.) cans tomatoes	1 c. raw rice (long-grain)

Brown beef in skillet and drain off fat. Put all ingredients in crockpot. Stir thoroughly. Cover and cook on low 6 to 8 hours or on high 4 hours.

CROCKPOT WILD RICE CASSEROLE EASY

1 lb. ground beef	1 can cream of mushroom soup
½ c. onion, chopped	1 can mushrooms
2 cans water	1 can chicken & rice soup
1 c. wild rice, rinsed	¼ c. soy sauce

Brown ground beef in skillet with onion, stirring until crumbly. Drain grease. Combine all ingredients and put in crockpot. Cook on low 12 hours.

BARBECUED HAMBURGERS

Onions	½ tsp. salt
3 T. salad oil	½ c. (or more) ketchup
2 lbs. ground beef patties	½ c. water
⅓ c. sugar	¼ c. (or more) vinegar
1 tsp. dry mustard	

Sauté onions in oil. Brown beef patties. Place onion and patties in crockpot. Mix remaining ingredients together and pour over patties and onions. Cook on low for at least 3 hours.

CHILIBURGERS EASY

1½ lbs. hamburger	¼ tsp. pepper
1 can chicken gumbo soup	½ tsp. paprika
½ tsp. salt	½ c. ketchup
½ tsp. chili powder	Onions to taste

Brown hamburger. Mix together with other ingredients. Cook in crockpot on low heat 1½ hours. Serve on buns.

CROCK-98

BARBECUED BEEF (EASY)

1 lb. ground beef
1 sm. onion, chopped
¼ c. water
2 T. flour

1 can corned beef
¼ c. brown sugar
3 T. vinegar
1 (17-oz.) bottle ketchup

Brown ground beef and onion. Drain off most of grease. Add remaining ingredients and place in crockpot. Cook on low 3 to 6 hours. Serve on buns.

SLOPPY JOES

3 lbs. ground beef
2 onions, finely chopped
1 green pepper, seeded & chopped (opt.)
2 (8-oz.) cans tomato sauce

2 pkgs. sloppy joe seasoning mix (opt.)
1 (8-oz.) can water
Salt to taste

Brown ground beef in skillet. Pour into colander; rinse well. Put into crockpot. Add onions, green pepper, tomato sauce, seasoning mix and water. Stir thoroughly. Salt to taste. Cover and cook on low 8 to 10 hours or on high 5 hours. Serve on buns. **Note:** If too much liquid, remove cover and set on high 30 minutes.

CROCKPOT LASAGNE

1½ lbs. ground beef
1 (16-oz.) box wide noodles
6 T. margarine
1 jar spaghetti sauce
1 sm. box pasteurized processed cheese (small chunks)

1 bag shredded mozzarella cheese

Brown meat. Cook noodles; drain. Add margarine to hot noodles; stir to melt. Layer all ingredients in crockpot, starting with noodles and cheese. Layer 3 times to fill crockpot. Pour a little sauce on top after finished layering. Turn crockpot to low for approximately 4 hours.

68

MAMA'S BEST LASAGNA

1 (32-oz.) can spaghetti sauce
  with mushrooms
1 egg
1 (12-oz.) ctn. cottage cheese or
  ricotta cheese
1 (10-oz.) pkg. broad noodles

12 oz. mozzarella cheese,
  shredded
1 lb. ground beef, browned
½ lb. Italian sausage,
  browned & crumbled
1 onion, chopped

Place enough spaghetti sauce on bottom of crockpot to cover bottom. Beat egg with cottage cheese or ricotta cheese. Start layering uncooked noodles, cottage or ricotta mix, mozzarella, sauce, meats and onion. Save a little mozzarella cheese to put on top. Turn crockpot to low and bake at least 5 hours. Can stay in crockpot on low for up to 10 hours.

LASAGNA IN WHITE SAUCE

1 lb. ground beef
1 onion, chopped
1 (14½-oz.) can diced tomatoes
2 T. tomato paste
1 beef bouillon cube
1½ tsp. Italian seasoning

1 tsp. salt
½ tsp. black pepper
¼ tsp. cayenne pepper
1 (8-oz.) pkg. mini lasagna
  noodles, cooked & drained

White Sauce:

2 T. margarine or butter, melted
3 T. all-purpose flour
1 tsp. salt
¼ tsp. black pepper

2 c. milk
2 c. mozzarella, shredded &
  divided

In a skillet brown ground beef and onion until onion is tender; drain fat. Transfer meat mixture to crockpot. Stir in tomatoes, tomato paste, bouillon and seasonings. Add cooked lasagna noodles. In a small bowl mix melted margarine, flour, salt, pepper, milk and 1 cup mozzarella cheese. Stir into crockpot. Cover and cook on low 4 to 6 hours or on high 2 to 3 hours. In the last 30 minutes, turn crockpot to high, if cooking on low. Top with remainder of mozzarella cheese. Serve when cheese is melted.

CROCKPOT PIZZA

1½ lbs. ground beef
Onion
Green pepper
1 (15-oz.) jar pizza sauce
1 (15-oz.) jar spaghetti sauce
1 pkg. egg noodles

8 oz. cheddar cheese, shredded
8 oz. mozzarella cheese,
  shredded
Sliced mushrooms
4 oz. pepperoni

Brown ground beef with onion and green pepper. Add both jars of sauce to meat. Cook noodles according to package. Put half of meat in crockpot. Layer with noodles, cheeses, mushrooms and pepperoni. Layer until all is used, ending with cheeses on top. Cook on high approximately 30 minutes or until cheese has melted.

OTHER BEEF DISHES

CORNED BEEF & CABBAGE (EASY)

3-4 lbs. corned beef brisket
2-3 onions, quartered

Cabbage, cut in sm. wedges
1-2 c. water

Put all ingredients in crockpot in order listed. Cover and set to high 7 to 10 hours. Push cabbage wedges down into liquid after 2 to 3 hours on high.

CORNED BEEF

Corned beef
Water
1 onion, quartered
1 stalk celery, scrubbed
1 clove garlic, peeled

5 whole allspice
½ bay leaf
1 carrot, pared
5 peppercorns
3 whole cloves

Unwrap, rinse and drain corned beef. Place in crockpot with water to cover. Add any of the remaining ingredients for an aromatic and flavored corned beef. Cover and cook on low 6 hours, until meat is fork tender. Drain meat and serve thinly sliced. Discard cooking vegetables. If desired, transfer cooking stock to large pot. Heat to boiling and use to cook cabbage wedges, about 7 minutes until tender. Serve with plain boiled potatoes.

GLAZED CORNED BEEF

1 bay leaf	3-4 lbs. corned beef (preferably
1 med. onion, sliced	round or rump cut)
2-3 strips fresh orange peel	3 T. frozen orange juice
(about 2 in. each)	concentrate, thawed
3 whole cloves	3 T. honey
1½ c. water	1 T. Dijon-style mustard

Combine bay leaf, onion, orange peel, cloves and water in crockpot. Add corned beef with fat side up. Cover and cook on low for 10 to 12 hours or on high for 5 to 6 hours or until fork tender. Remove meat from broth. Score top of corned beef in diamond shapes. Insert additional cloves to decorate. About 30 minutes before serving, place corned beef on heat-proof platter. For glaze, mix together orange juice concentrate, honey and mustard until smooth and blended. Spoon over corned beef. Bake in 375° oven for 20 to 30 minutes, basting occasionally.

BEEF & EGG CASSEROLE (EASY)

2 c. uncooked elbow macaroni	1½ c. cheddar cheese, cubed
2 (10-oz.) cans cream of	1 T. butter or margarine
mushroom soup	4 hard-cooked eggs, diced
1 (5-oz.) jar or 2 (3-oz.) pkgs.	½ med. onion, chopped
sliced dried beef, shredded	2 c. evaporated milk

Combine all ingredients in crockpot; stir thoroughly. Cover and cook on low 5 to 7 hours or on high 3 hours.

VEAL SCALLOPINI IN CROCKPOT

2 lbs. veal cubes	1 onion, chopped
¾ c. flour seasoned with 1 tsp.	1½ tsp. salt
salt & ¼ tsp. pepper	1 tsp. sugar
¼ c. oil	½ tsp. oregano
1 (4-oz.) can sliced mushrooms	1 sm. clove garlic, diced
(with juice)	1 (1-lb.) can tomatoes

Roll veal cubes in seasoned flour and fry in hot oil until well browned. Put into crockpot. Add all remaining ingredients. Stir together well. Cover and cook on low 6 to 8 hours. Serve over rice or fettuccini. (Can be mixed together the night before and put in crockpot in morning.)

CROCK-98

WORKING WOMAN'S VEAL SCALLOPINI

1 (12-oz.) jar marinara sauce
1 (16-oz.) jar traditional-style
  Italian cooking sauce
1 (14-oz.) jar beef & pork pasta
  sauce

1 sm. can sliced mushrooms
1 med. onion, sliced or diced
3 lbs. veal cubes for stew
1 (1-lb.) box cut ziti macaroni (or
  use 1 lb. spaghetti)

Put all ingredients except pasta in crockpot. Cook on low 8 hours. Cook pasta al dente (11 minutes for ziti) and serve. Can also serve scallopini with mashed potatoes.

SLOW COOKER LIVER

2 lbs. liver
4 strips bacon
1 sm. onion
½ c. celery, chopped

½ c. carrots, chopped
1 can stewed tomatoes
½ tsp. salt
⅛ tsp. pepper

Arrange liver in crockpot. Cut strips of bacon in half and arrange on top of liver. Slice onion and put on top of bacon. Mix remaining ingredients and pour over all. Cover and cook on low 6 to 8 hours.

CROCK-98

PORK COOKERY

ROAST

PORK ROAST *EASY*

Pork roast
1 c. water
¼ c. wine

1 onion, halved
½ c. + 2 T. soy sauce
2-3 T. brown sugar

Combine all ingredients in crockpot and cook 6 to 8 hours. May add brown sugar just before serving.

ZESTY ROAST PORK *EASY*

1 pork blade roast
Dijon mustard
Salt
Pepper

2 T. fresh garlic, minced
1 T. celery flakes
1 tsp. rosemary

Place roast, fat side down, in crockpot. Brush roast with Dijon mustard. Sprinkle with salt and pepper. Coat with garlic. Sprinkle with celery flakes and rosemary. Cook all day on low.

CROCK-98

PORK ROAST

4 to 5-lb. pork roast
Salt & pepper to taste
Garlic salt or garlic (opt.)
2 med. onions, sliced

2 bay leaves
1 clove (opt.)
1 c. hot water
2 T. soy sauce

Rub roast with salt and pepper. Make slits in meat for garlic salt or garlic. Insert garlic cloves or garlic salt into slits. Place roast in broiler pan and broil 15 to 20 minutes until brown. Put 1 onion in bottom of crockpot, then roast and top with remaining onion, bay leaves, clove, water and soy sauce. Cook on low 10 hours or on high approximately 5 hours.

CRANBERRY PORK ROAST

3 to 4-lb. pork roast
Salt & pepper to taste
1 c. ground cranberries
1/4 c. honey

1 tsp. orange peel, grated
1/8 tsp. ground cloves
1/8 tsp. ground nutmeg

Brown roast. Place roast in crockpot. Stir together remaining ingredients and pour over roast. Cook on low in crockpot 8 to 10 hours or until tender.

CHILE VERDE PORK ROAST

3 lbs. pork butt roast, cut into
  cubes
Salt, pepper & garlic to taste
2 T. oil
1 lg. can tomatoes, mashed

1 (7-oz.) can chilies, diced
1 (7-oz.) can salsa
1 lg. onion, diced
Flour tortillas

Cover meat with salt, pepper and garlic. Sauté in oil. Do not brown. Add to crockpot. Add tomatoes, chilies, salsa and onion to crockpot and cook all day. Serve with slotted spoon into warmed flour tortillas. Fold up and ladle juice over top.

INDONESIAN PORK

4 to 5-lb. boneless pork roast
Salt & pepper to taste
1 c. hot water
¼ c. molasses

¼ c. prepared mustard
¼ c. vinegar
¼ c. orange marmalade
¼ tsp. ground ginger

Place meat rack in bottom of crockpot. Sprinkle roast with salt and pepper. Place on rack in pot. Pour hot water around roast. Cover and cook on low 8 to 10 hours or until done. Remove meat from pot and place on an ovenproof platter. Combine remaining ingredients and brush over cooked pork. Brown in a 400° oven for 30 minutes. Brush several times with sauce. (Basting sauce can be doubled and served over rice.)

SLOW COOKED CARNITAS

3 to 4-lb. pork roast, blade or
  shoulder
1 c. green chile salsa

1 tsp. garlic powder
Warm tortillas

Opt. Garnishes:

Shredded lettuce
Chopped tomatoes
Sliced green onions
Shredded cheese

Chopped avocado
Sliced black olives
Sour cream

Trim roast of excess fat. Place in crockpot. Pour salsa over top and sprinkle on garlic powder. Cook 8 to 10 hours on low. Drain off fat. Remove bones and tear meat into shreds. Place on warm platter or back into warm crockpot. Serve with warm tortillas and your choice of garnishes.

POLYNESIAN BAR-B-Q PORK (EASY)

½ c. soy sauce
¼ c. dry sherry
½ c. brown sugar
2 cloves garlic, crushed
⅛ tsp. pepper

½ c. BBQ sauce
1 (8-oz.) can pineapple chunks,
  undrained
2-lb. extra-lean pork or pork
  tenderloin, cut in strips

Combine all ingredients except pork strips in crockpot; stir well. Add pork strips and stir to coat thoroughly. Cover and cook on low 4 to 6 hours. Serve with a small dish of sauce for dunking and rice.

CROCK-98

SWEET & SOUR CANTONESE PORK

2 lbs. lean pork shoulders, cut
  into strips
1 green pepper, seeded & cut
  into strips
½ med. onion, thinly sliced
¼ c. brown sugar, packed
2 T. cornstarch

2 c. pineapple chunks (reserve
  juice)
¼ c. cider vinegar
¼ c. water
1 T. soy sauce
½ tsp. salt

Place pork strips in crockpot. Add green pepper and sliced onion. In bowl mix brown sugar and cornstarch. Add 1 cup reserved pineapple juice, vinegar, water, soy sauce and salt; blend until smooth. Pour over meat and vegetables. Cover and cook on low 7 to 9 hours. One hour before serving, add pineapple chunks; stir. Serve over chow mein noodles or rice.

DOWN SOUTH BARBECUE PORK

2 onions, sliced
4 to 5-lb. pork roast or fresh
  picnic ham
5-6 cloves

2 c. water
1 lg. onion, chopped
1 (16-oz.) bottle barbecue sauce

Put half of sliced onions in bottom of crockpot, then add meat, cloves and water. Put remaining sliced onion on top. Cover and cook overnight or 8 to 12 hours on low. Remove bone and fat from meat. Put meat back in crockpot. Add chopped onion and barbecue sauce. Cover and cook an additional 3 to 5 hours on high or 8 to 12 hours on low, stirring 2 or 3 times. Serve from crockpot on large buns.

PORK CHOPS

EASY PORK CHOPS

6-8 pork chops
Salt
Pepper
Flour

Cooking oil
1 pkg. dry onion or mushroom
  soup mix
1 c. water

Coat pork chops with salt, pepper and flour. Brown in oil in skillet. Layer dry onion soup mix and pork chops in crockpot. Add 1 cup water. Cook on low 6 to 8 hours.

CREAMY PORK CHOPS

4-6 pork chops
2 cans cream of mushroom
  soup

1 can milk

Brown pork chops; lightly seasoning to taste. Place in crockpot. Mix soup with milk and pour over chops. Cook all day on low. Serve with steamed rice.

FINGER LICKIN' GOOD PORK CHOPS

6-8 lean pork chops, 1-in. thick
½ c. flour
1 T. salt
1½ tsp. dry mustard

½ tsp. garlic powder
2 T. oil
1 can chicken & rice soup

Dredge pork chops in mixture of flour, salt, dry mustard and garlic powder. Brown in oil in large skillet. Place browned pork chops in crockpot. Add soup. Cover and cook on low 6 to 8 hours or on high 3½ hours.

CROCK-98

COUNTRY PORK CHOPS

6-8 pork chops
10 oz. mixed vegetables
2 c. water
1 can cream of celery soup
1 can mushrooms

1 box scalloped potatoes &
  sauce mix
½ c. milk
1 tsp. salt
½ tsp. Worcestershire sauce

Brown chops. Place in crockpot. Boil vegetables in water for 10 minutes. Add soup, mushrooms, potatoes and sauce mix, milk, salt and Worcestershire sauce; mix well. Place mixture in crockpot with browned chops. Cook on high approximately 1 hour or on low for several hours. Cook until chops and potatoes are tender.

PORK CHOP SURPRISE (EASY)

4-5 med. potatoes, washed,
  pared & sliced
3-4 carrots, sliced
3-4 stalks celery, sliced

1 lg. (or 2 sm.) onions, diced
5-6 pork chops
1 can cream of mushroom soup

Place potatoes, carrots, celery and onions in bottom of crockpot. Place pork chops on top of vegetables. Pour soup over top. **Do not use water.** Cook on low heat 8 to 10 hours. Serve over noodles.

APPLES, SAUERKRAUT & PORK CHOPS

4 pork chops
Oil
1 med. onions, sliced in rings
1-2 cloves garlic, crushed
¾ c. apple juice
3 c. sauerkraut, drained

1½ tsp. caraway seed
¼ tsp. salt
¼ tsp. pepper
¼ tsp. thyme
1 red apple, sliced

In a skillet brown pork chops in oil. In crockpot place half of onion, garlic, apple juice, sauerkraut and seasonings. Put chops on top. Then add remaining onion, garlic, apple juice, sauerkraut and seasonings. Top with apple slices. Cover and cook on low 6 to 8 hours or on high 4 hours.

CROCK-98

STUFFED PORK CHOPS

4 double pork loin chops, well
  trimmed
Salt & pepper
1 (12-oz.) can whole-kernel corn,
  drained
1 sm. onion, chopped
1 sm. green pepper, seeded &
  chopped

1 c. fresh bread crumbs
½ tsp. leaf oregano or leaf sage
⅓ c. raw, long-grain converted
  rice
1 (8-oz.) can tomato sauce

Cut a pocket in each chop, cutting from the edge almost to the bone. Lightly season pockets with salt and pepper. In bowl combine all ingredients except pork chops and tomato sauce. Pack vegetable mixture into pockets. Secure along fat side with wooden picks. Pour any remaining vegetable mixture into crockpot. Moisten top surface of each chop with tomato sauce. Add stuffed pork chops to crockpot, stacking to fit if necessary. Pour any remaining tomato sauce on top. Cover and cook on low 8 to 10 hours or on high 4 to 5 hours, until done. To serve, remove pork chops to heatproof platter and mound vegetable-rice mixture in center.

CHOP SUEY (EASY)

2-3 pork shoulder chops, boned,
  well trimmed & diced
2 c. cooked or raw chicken,
  cubed
½ c. chicken broth
1 c. celery, diagonally sliced
2 tsp. soy sauce

½ tsp. sugar
Salt
1½ c. water chestnuts, thinly
  sliced
1½ c. bamboo shoots, in
  julienne strips

Combine all ingredients in crockpot; stir well. Cover and cook on low 8 to 10 hours or on high 4 to 5 hours.

PORK STEAKS

CANTONESE DINNER

1½ lbs. pork steak, ½ in. thick, cut into strips
2 T. oil
1 lg. onion, sliced
1 sm. green pepper, cut into strips
1 (4-oz.) can mushrooms, drained
¾ c. evaporated milk
1 (8-oz.) can tomato sauce
3 T. brown sugar
1½ T. vinegar
1½ tsp. salt
2 tsp. Worcestershire sauce

Brown pork strips in oil in skillet to remove excess fat. Drain on a doubled paper towel. Place pork strips and all remaining ingredients into crockpot. Cover and cook on low 6 to 8 hours or on high 4 hours. Serve over hot, fluffy rice.

SWEET & SOUR PORK STEAKS

4-6 pork shoulder steaks
1 T. cooking oil
1 (15-oz.) can crushed pineapple
½ c. green pepper, chopped
½ c. water
⅓ c. brown sugar
2 T. ketchup
1 T. quick-cooking tapioca
3 tsp. soy sauce
½ tsp. dry mustard

In a skillet brown pork steaks on both sides in hot oil; drain fat. Transfer to crockpot. In a bowl combine pineapple, green pepper, water, brown sugar, ketchup, tapioca, soy sauce and dry mustard. Pour over pork steaks. Cover and cook on low 8 to 10 hours or on high 4 to 5 hours. Serve over rice, if desired.

HAM

HOMESTYLE HAM

1 ham
1 sm. glass cola (not diet)

1 c. brown sugar
1 can crushed pineapple

Place ham in crockpot on high. Combine cola, sugar and crushed pineapple in saucepan. Bring to boil over medium-high heat. Pour over ham. Cook 6 to 8 hours.

BARBECUE HAM SANDWICHES (EASY)

1 qt. ketchup
½ c. molasses
½ c. brown sugar

1 tsp. liquid smoke
½ c. barbecue sauce
Shredded ham

Mix all ingredients except ham. Heat on stove until hot and blended. Place ham in crockpot. Pour sauce over ham. Cook several hours on low.

SCALLOPED POTATOES & HAM

8-10 potatoes, sliced
1 lg. onion, diced
3 c. ham, cubed

2-3 c. cheese, shredded
2 (8-oz.) cans mushroom soup

In crockpot layer potatoes, onion, ham and cheese. Top with 1 can mushroom soup. Turn crockpot to high. After 15 minutes to ½ hour, add second can of mushroom soup to thicken. Cook on high 4 to 6 hours or low 8 to 10 hours.

SPICY BRAISED HAM

2-2½ lbs. smoked boneless
  pork shoulder butt
2 c. water
6 whole cloves

1 bay leaf
4 whole peppercorns
1 stalk celery, cut up
1 carrot, pared & sliced

Put all ingredients in crockpot. Cover and cook on low 6 to 8 hours or on high 3 to 4 hours. Drain and serve.

CROCK-98

VEGETABLE-PORK DINNER

¼ c. margarine
½ green pepper, diced
¼ c. flour
½ tsp. paprika
¾ tsp. salt
¼ tsp. pepper
⅛ tsp. thyme & marjoram
2 c. milk

1 (8-oz.) can cream-style corn
1 (8-oz.) can green peas
2 c. potatoes, diced, cooked
1 med. onion, diced
2 c. ham, diced, cooked
½ tsp. dry mustard
1 c. sharp cheddar cheese, shredded

Melt margarine in saucepan. Add green pepper and sauté. Stir in flour and seasonings. Gradually stir in milk and cook until thick. Add to crockpot with all remaining ingredients. Stir well. Cover and cook on low 6 to 8 hours. Serve with hot rolls and salad.

HAM & LIMA BEANS

1 lb. dry lima beans, soaked overnight
1 lg. onion, chopped
1 lg. green pepper, chopped
1 tsp. dry mustard
1 tsp. salt

1 tsp. pepper
¼-½ lb. ham or bacon, cut in sm. pieces
1 c. water
1 can tomato soup

Put all ingredients in crockpot. Stir together well. Cover and cook on low 7 to 10 hours or on high 4 to 5 hours. Serve with wedges of hot cornbread.

HAM STEAK IN PORT WINE

2 ham slices, each about ¾ in. thick
1 c. sweet cider
1 c. port wine (opt.)
½ c. maple syrup
¾ c. cranberries
¾ c. seedless grapes (or raisins)

6 slices pineapple (opt.)
4 whole cloves
Juice of 1 orange
2 T. cornstarch
3 T. water

Place ham slices in crockpot. (Roll to fit, if necessary.) Add remaining ingredients except cornstarch and water. Cover and cook on high 1 hour, then on low 6 hours. To thicken gravy: Set crockpot on high. Remove ham slices. Make a paste of cornstarch and water. Stir into crockpot. Cook on high until thick.

CROCK-98

HAM TETRAZZINI   *EASY*

1 (10¾-oz.) can condensed
  cream of mushroom soup
½ c. evaporated or scalded milk
1½ tsp. prepared horseradish
½ c. grated Romano or
  Parmesan cheese
1-1½ c. cooked ham, cubed

½ c. stuffed olives, sliced (opt.)
1 (4-oz.) can sliced mushrooms,
  drained
¼ c. dry sherry or dry white
  wine
1 (5-oz.) pkg. spaghetti
2 T. butter, melted

Combine all ingredients except spaghetti and butter in crockpot; stir well. Cover and cook on low 6 to 8 hours. Just before serving, cook spaghetti according to package directions; drain and toss with butter. Stir in crockpot. Sprinkle additional grated cheese over top.

FRUITED HAM LOAF

¾ c. dried fruit bits
2 T. apple butter
1 egg, beaten
¼ c. milk
½ c. graham cracker crumbs
½ tsp. black pepper

1 lb. ground fully cooked ham
½ lb. ground pork
½ c. packed brown sugar
2 T. apple juice
½ tsp. dry mustard

In a small bowl combine fruit bits and apple butter. In a large bowl combine egg, milk, graham cracker crumbs, pepper, ground ham and ground pork. On top of waxed paper, pat half of the meat mixture into a 7-inch circle. Spread fruit mixture on meat circle to within 1 inch of edges. Top with remaining meat mixture. Press edge of meat to seal well. Lift meat off of waxed paper and transfer to crockpot. Press meat away from sides of crockpot to avoid excess browning. Cover and cook on low 8 to 10 hours or on high 4 to 6 hours. Loaf is done when meat thermometer inserted reads 170°. In a small bowl combine brown sugar, apple juice and dry mustard. Spread over meat. Cover and cook on low or high heat for 30 minutes more. Carefully lift ham loaf from crockpot and transfer to serving plate.

PORK RIBS

SAVORY BARBECUED SPARERIBS (EASY)

3-4 lbs. pork spareribs
3 c. ketchup
1 T. Worcestershire sauce

2 T. Dijon mustard
2 T. brown sugar
1 tsp. black pepper

Place spareribs on bottom of crockpot. In medium bowl combine ketchup, Worcestershire sauce, mustard, sugar and pepper. Cover spare ribs with mixture. Cook on low 6 to 8 hours.

SPARERIBS SUPREME

3 lbs. country-style spareribs
¼ c. onion, chopped
¼ c. celery, chopped
1 c. ketchup
½ c. water
¼ c. lemon juice

2 T. brown sugar
3 T. Worcestershire sauce
2 T. vinegar
1 T. prepared mustard
½ tsp. salt
¼ tsp. pepper

Brown ribs. Add ribs and all other ingredients to crockpot. Simmer on low 8 to 9 hours.

CABBAGE 'N KRAUT SPARERIBS

3-4 lbs. lean pork spareribs, cut
  in serving pieces
Salt & pepper to taste
1 sm. can sauerkraut
½ sm. head cabbage, thinly
  sliced
1 lg. onion, thinly sliced

1 apple, cored & sliced
1 tsp. salt
1 tsp. caraway seeds or dill
  weed
1 c. water

Sprinkle spareribs with salt and pepper. Brown 30 minutes in heavy skillet or broiler pan. Place alternate layers of spareribs, sauerkraut, cabbage, onion and apple in crockpot. Add salt and caraway seeds or dill weed to water and pour over all. Cover and cook on low 6 to 8 hours or on high 4 to 5 hours. (Stir several times during cooking when using high.) **Note:** May be prepared using all sauerkraut or all cabbage, if desired.

CROCK-98

HONIED PORK RIBS & RICE

2 lbs. extra-lean back ribs
1 (10½-oz.) can condensed beef
  consommé
½ c. water
2 T. maple syrup

2 T. honey
3 T. soy sauce
2 T. barbecue sauce
½ tsp. dry mustard
1½ c. quick-cooking rice

If ribs are fatty, place on broiler rack and broil 15 to 20 minutes; drain well. Otherwise, wash ribs and pat dry. Cut ribs into single servings. Combine remaining ingredients except rice in crockpot; stir to mix. Add ribs. Cover and cook on low 8 to 10 hours or on high 4 to 5 hours. Remove ribs and keep warm. Turn crockpot to high. Add quick-cooking rice and cook until done. Serve rice on warm platter surrounded by ribs.

PORK SAUSAGE

OLD WORLD SAUERKRAUT SUPPER

3 strips bacon, cut into sm.
  pieces
1½ T. flour
2 lg. cans sauerkraut
2 sm. potatoes, cubed
2 sm. apples, cubed

3 T. brown sugar
1½ tsp. caraway seeds
3 lbs. Polish sausage, cut up
  into pieces
½ c. water

Fry bacon until crisp; drain. Add flour to bacon drippings and blend well. Stir in sauerkraut; mix well. Place sauerkraut mixture and bacon pieces in crockpot. Add remaining ingredients; stir together thoroughly. Cover and cook on low 7 to 9 hours or on high 3 to 4 hours.

BARBECUE POLISH SAUSAGE (EASY)

3 lbs. Polish sausage
1 c. barbecue sauce

1 c. ketchup
¾ c. brown sugar

Cut sausage into pieces. Put in crockpot. Add other ingredients; simmer until ready to eat.

SLOW POT POLISH SAUSAGE & CABBAGE

½ lg. head cabbage, sliced & shredded
2 sm. potatoes, pared & diced
1 tsp. salt
½ tsp. caraway seeds

1 lg. onion, thinly sliced
1½ lbs. Polish sausage, cut into ½-in. pieces
1 can chicken broth

Place all ingredients into crockpot; stir well. Cover and cook on low 6 to 10 hours. Serve with mustard and boiled new potatoes.

CROCK-98

POULTRY COOKERY

CHICKEN

EASY CHICKEN (EASY)

2 to 3-lb. chicken
Water
2 T. apple cider vinegar

1 c. Italian dressing

Place chicken in a large pot. Cover with water. Add vinegar and soak chicken for 30 minutes. Rinse chicken and place in crockpot. Pour Italian dressing over chicken. Cook 4 hours on high or 8 to 12 hours on low. **Option:** Place a few carrots, potatoes, celery and onions in bottom of crockpot. Add 1 cup water. Place chicken on top and top with dressing.

ITALIAN CHICKEN BREASTS (EASY)

5 skinless, boneless chicken
breasts
1 sm. bottle low fat Italian
dressing

½ c. butter, melted

Combine chicken, dressing and butter in crockpot. Cook on low 6 to 7 hours.

CROCK-98

FLAVORFUL CHICKEN

3 to 4-lb. roasting chicken
Salt & pepper
Parsley

Butter
Basil or tarragon (opt.)

Thoroughly wash chicken and pat dry. Sprinkle chicken cavity gener-ously with salt, pepper and parsley; place in crockpot, breast up. Dot breast with butter. Sprinkle with parsley and basil or tarragon, if desired. Cover and cook on high 1 hour, then turn to low 8 to 10 hours.

EASY HERB CHICKEN

3-5 lbs. chicken, cut-up
¾ c. salad dressing
¾ c. Parmesan cheese

1 tsp. oregano
1 tsp. basil

Skin chicken and place in crockpot. Combine salad dressing, cheese, oregano and basil. Spread over the top. (If you layer the chicken, place some sauce between layers.) Bake in a crockpot 8 hours on low or 4 hours on high.

TARRAGON CHICKEN

4-lb. roasting chicken
Seasoned salt
Seasoned pepper
Parsley, finely chopped

3 T. margarine, melted
1 tsp. dried tarragon, crushed
⅔ c. dry white wine

Wash and pat chicken thoroughly dry. Sprinkle inside and out with seasoned salt, seasoned pepper and parsley. Put chicken in crockpot, breast side up. Brush with melted margarine. Sprinkle with tarragon. Pour wine into crockpot. Set on high. Cover and cook 1 hour, then turn to low and cook 8 to 10 hours.

ZESTY CHICKEN

½ c. tomato juice
½ c. soy sauce
½ c. sugar

½ c. oil
3 cloves garlic, minced
3 lg. chicken breasts

Mix juice, soy sauce, sugar, oil and garlic. Dip chicken in mixture. Place chicken in crockpot. Pour remaining sauce in crockpot. Cook 6 to 8 hours on low or 3 to 4 hours on high.

LEMON ROAST CHICKEN

3-lb. whole broiler or 3 lbs.
  chicken breasts
Salt & pepper
1 tsp. dried oregano,
  crumbled & divided

2 cloves garlic, minced and
  divided
2 T. butter
¼ c. sherry or water
3 T. lemon juice

Wash chicken and giblets; pat dry. Season with salt and pepper. Sprinkle half the oregano and half the garlic inside chicken cavity. Melt butter in large frying pan. Brown chicken on all sides. Transfer to crockpot. Sprinkle with remaining seasonings. Add sherry or water to frying pan. Stir to loosen brown bits. Pour into crockpot. Cover; cook on low 8 hours. Add lemon juice the last hour of cooking. When done, transfer chicken to carving board if using whole chicken. Skim fat off juice and pour juices into sauce bowl. Carve bird. Serve with juice spooned over chicken.

CHICKEN PARMESAN EASY

4 boneless, skinless chicken
  breasts
2 cans cream of chicken soup
¾ c. fresh Parmesan cheese,
  grated

¼-½ c. water
Salt & pepper to taste

Combine all ingredients in crockpot. Cook all day on low or 2 hours on high. Serve over vermicelli noodles.

CHICKEN WITH CREAM OF CELERY SOUP

4 (or more) chicken breasts
Water
Salt & pepper

2 cans cream of celery soup
Paprika
2 tsp. margarine

Skin chicken and cook in water with salt and pepper until tender. Remove chicken from bones. Put 1 can soup in crockpot. Sprinkle chicken with salt, pepper and paprika. Place chicken in crockpot and put margarine on top. Add second can of soup; mix well. May need to add ½ can of water. Cook on low 6 to 8 hours.

CHICKEN DELUXE

4-6 boneless chicken breasts
1 can cream of chicken soup
1 can cream of celery soup

1 tsp. curry powder
1 tsp. turmeric
Salt & pepper to taste

Place chicken in crockpot. Pour the soups and seasonings over chicken. Cook all day on low. May add pared and diced potatoes.

COUNTRY CHICKEN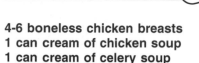

1 fryer, cut-up
1 env. dry onion soup mix
1 can cream of chicken soup

1 can cream of mushroom soup
1 soup can water

Place chicken in crockpot. Sprinkle soup mix over it. Add soups and water. Cook on low 6 to 8 hours. Serve over rice.

CHICKEN & GRAVY EASY

6 chicken breasts
½ jar dried beef
2 T. bacon bits

1 can cream of mushroom soup
1 c. sour cream
½ c. water

Combine all ingredients in crockpot. Cook on low 8 hours. Serve over rice.

CROCK-98

BARBECUE CHICKEN

14-16 sm. chicken legs & wings

1 bottle barbecue sauce
2-3 T. water

Wash chicken well. Layer in crockpot evenly. Pour barbecue sauce and water on chicken. Cook on high 4 to 5 hours.

SHAKEN BARBECUE CHICKEN

1 chicken, cut into serving
pieces
1 box barbecue-style baking
coating mix

Onion, sliced
1/2 c. water

Coat chicken with mix. Place in crockpot. Top with onion and add water. Cover and cook on low 4 to 5 hours.

BBQ CHICKEN IN A CROCKPOT

1 whole chicken, cut up &
skinned
1 bottle barbecue sauce
1/2 sm. onion, chopped

Salt & pepper to taste
1/8 c. white wine
1 T. dry mustard
1 T. brown sugar

Combine all ingredients in crockpot. Cook 8 hours on low.

CHICKEN PARISIENNE

6 med. chicken breasts
Salt & pepper (opt.)
Paprika
1 (10 1/2-oz.) can cream of
mushroom soup

1 (4-oz.) can sliced mushrooms,
drained
1 c. sour cream mixed with 1/4 c.
flour

Sprinkle chicken breasts with salt, pepper and paprika. Place in crock-pot. Mix soup and mushrooms until well combined. Pour over chicken in crockpot. Cover and cook on low 6 to 8 hours or on high 2 1/2 to 3 1/2 hours, adding sour cream mixed with flour during the last 30 minutes. Serve sauce over chicken with rice or noodles.

CROCK-98

CHICKEN SUPREME

1 chicken (whole or cut up)
1 can cream of mushroom soup
½ pkg. dry onion soup mix
½ can water

1 c. sour cream
1 T. flour
Mushrooms (opt.)

Put chicken in crockpot. Mix soup, soup mix and water together. Pour over chicken. Turn crockpot on high and cook for 1 hour, then turn to low and cook all day. 30 minutes before serving, remove chicken. Mix sour cream and flour together and add to the gravy. Serve over rice or potatoes. Add extra mushrooms, if desired.

BAKED CHICKEN & MUSHROOMS

1 pkg. dried beef
6-8 chicken breasts
6-8 slices bacon

1 (10-oz.) can cream of
  mushroom soup
¼ c. sour cream
¼ c. flour

Arrange dried beef on bottom of greased crockpot. Wrap each chicken breast with a strip of bacon. Lay on top of dried beef. Mix soup, sour cream and flour. Pour over chicken. Cover and cook on low 8 to 10 hours or on high 3 to 5 hours. Serve over hot buttered noodles.

BACON-WRAPPED CHICKEN

8 boneless chicken breasts
8 slices ham
8 strips bacon
1 can mushroom soup
½-1 c. sour cream

1 (4-oz.) can mushrooms,
  drained
Green onions
Salt & pepper

Place each chicken breast on a piece of ham, then wrap each breast with a bacon strip and place in crockpot. Combine undiluted soup, sour cream, mushrooms and onions. Place over chicken breasts. Season with salt and pepper. Cook on high 3 to 5 hours. Serve with rice pilaf and steamed vegetables.

CHICKEN TORTILLAS

1 fryer, cooked & boned
1 (10-oz.) can cream of chicken
  soup
½ c. tomatoes & chilies

2 T. quick-cooking tapioca
6-8 tortillas, torn into pieces
1 med. onion, chopped
2 c. cheddar cheese, grated

Cut chicken into bite-sized pieces. Mix well with soup, tomatoes and chilies and tapioca. Line bottom of crockpot with ⅓ of tortillas. Add ⅓ of chicken and soup mixture; sprinkle with ⅓ of onion and cheese. Repeat layers of tortillas, chicken, soup mixture, onions and cheese 2 times. Cover and cook on low 6 to 8 hours or on high 3 hours.

CHICKEN ENCHILADAS

4 boneless, skinless chicken
  breasts
1 (4-oz.) can chopped green
  chilies
2 (14-oz.) cans cream of
  mushroom soup

8-10 corn tortillas
1 c. cheddar cheese, shredded
Sour cream, salsa & olives

Combine chicken breasts, chilies and soup in crockpot. Cook on low 4½ hours, stirring each hour. Preheat oven to 350°. Remove chicken breasts. Cut into bite-sized pieces. Place chicken on tortillas, dividing equally. Roll up tortillas, enclosing chicken. Place in baking dish. Spoon mushroom sauce from crockpot over tortillas to cover. Top with cheese. Bake 15 to 20 minutes. Garnish with sour cream, salsa and olives.

ARROZ CON POLO

3-4 lbs. chicken, cut up
Salt, pepper & paprika to taste
1 lg. onion, chopped
1 sm. green pepper, chopped
2 sm. garlic cloves, minced
1 sm. can pimiento, diced
¼-½ tsp. chili powder

2 chicken bouillon cubes
¼-½ lb. precooked pork
  sausages (or 1 c. diced ham)
1 (1-lb., 14-oz.) can tomatoes
1 c. raw long grain rice
1 (10-oz.) pkg. frozen peas

Season chicken pieces with salt, pepper and paprika. Put all ingredients except rice and peas in crockpot. Cover and cook on low 6 to 8 hours or on high 4 hours. Turn to high 1 to 2 hours before serving. Add rice and peas. Cover and continue cooking on high until rice is tender. Stir occasionally.

CHICKEN & RICE CASSEROLE

4 lg. chicken breasts
1 sm. can cream of chicken
  soup
1 sm. can cream of celery soup

1 sm. can cream of mushroom
  soup
½ c. water
1 c. long-grain rice
½ c. celery, diced

Combine in crockpot the soups, water and rice. Place the chicken on top, then add the diced celery. Cook for 1½ to 2 hours on high or 4 hours on low.

CHUNKY CHICKEN WITH RICE

4 pcs. skinless, boneless
  chicken
1 can creamy onion soup

1 can cream of chicken or
  cream of celery soup

Place chicken and both cans of soup in crockpot. Cook on low 8 hours or on high 4 hours. Serve over rice.

CROCKPOT CHICKEN

1 c. long-grain rice
1 can cream of mushroom soup
1 can cream of chicken soup
1 can cream of celery soup
1 can water
1 whole cut-up chicken or 4
  chicken breasts

¼ c. French dressing
¼ c. butter, melted
Onion (opt.)
Salt, to taste

Combine in crockpot rice, soups and water. Add chicken, French dressing, butter, onion, if desired, and salt. Cook on low 8 hours or high 4 hours. If cooked on high, rice must be stirred up from bottom.

CROCK-98

TERIYAKI CHICKEN

3 lg. chicken breasts, with ribs still attached (thighs can be used)
1 (16-oz.) can pineapple chunks, partially drained

3 c. teriyaki sauce
Your choice of vegetables (broccoli recommended)

Place chicken in crockpot. Pour in pineapple. Add teriyaki sauce and vegetables. Cook on low 6 to 8 hours or high 3 to 4 hours. Serve over rice.

ORIENTAL CHICKEN

1 chicken, cut up or chicken breasts
1/3 c. soy sauce
2 T. dry sherry
1 tsp. dry ginger or 2 tsp. fresh ginger

1 clove garlic, minced
2 T. brown sugar
2 T. cornstarch
2 T. cold water
1/4 c. slivered almonds

Place chicken in crockpot. Mix soy sauce, sherry, ginger, garlic and brown sugar. Pour over chicken. Cook on low 8 hours. Gravy may be made by thickening sauce with cornstarch, then adding cold water and slivered almonds. Serve gravy over chicken. Garnish with additional almonds.

ALMOND CHICKEN

1 (14-oz.) can chicken broth
1 slice bacon, diced
2 T. butter
3/4-1 lb. boned chicken breasts, cut into 1-in. pieces
1 1/2 c. celery, diagonally sliced
1 sm. onion, sliced

1 (4-oz.) can sliced mushrooms, drained
2 T. soy sauce
1/2 tsp. salt
Fluffy rice
2/3 c. slivered almonds, toasted

Pour chicken broth into crockpot. Cover and turn crockpot to high. In skillet heat bacon and butter. Add chicken pieces and brown quickly on all sides. With slotted spoon, move browned chicken to crockpot. Quickly sauté celery, onion and mushrooms in skillet until just slightly limp. Add contents of skillet to crockpot with soy sauce and salt; stir well. Cover and cook on low 6 to 8 hours or on high 3 to 4 hours. Serve over hot, fluffy rice and garnish with toasted almonds.

CROCK-98

CHICKEN A LA ORANGE

3 whole chicken breasts, halved
2/3 c. flour
1 tsp. salt
1 tsp. nutmeg
1/2 tsp. cinnamon
Dash of pepper
Dash of garlic powder
2-3 sweet potatoes, pared & cut
  into 1/4-in. slices

1 (10¾-oz.) can condensed
  cream of celery or cream of
  mushroom soup
1 (4-oz.) can sliced mushrooms,
  drained
1/2 c. orange juice
1/2 tsp. orange rind, grated
2 tsp. brown sugar
3 T. flour
Buttered rice

Rinse chicken breasts and pat dry. Combine 2/3 cup flour with salt, nutmeg, cinnamon, pepper and garlic powder. Thoroughly coat chicken in flour mixture. Place sweet potato slices in bottom of crockpot. Place chicken breasts on top. Combine soup with mushrooms, orange juice, rind, sugar and 3 tablespoons flour; stir well. Pour soup mixture over chicken breasts. Cover and cook on low 8 to 10 hours or on high 3 to 4 hours or until chicken and vegetables are tender. Serve chicken and sauce over hot, buttered rice.

ALPINE CHICKEN

2 tsp. chicken bouillon granules
1 T. fresh parsley, chopped
3/4 tsp. poultry seasoning
1/3 c. Canadian bacon, diced
2-3 carrots, thinly sliced
1-2 stalks celery, thinly sliced
1 sm. onion, thinly sliced

1/4 c. water
1 (3-lb.) broiler chicken, cut up
  (may substitute boneless,
  skinless chicken breasts)
1 (11-oz.) can condensed
  cheddar cheese soup
1 T. all-purpose flour

In a small bowl mix bouillon granules, chopped parsley and poultry seasoning; set aside. Layer in crockpot in order: Canadian bacon, carrots, celery and onion. Add water. Remove skin and excess fat from chicken; rinse and pat dry. Place white meat in crockpot. Sprinkle with half of reserved seasoning mixture. Top with remaining chicken and sprinkle with remaining mixture. Stir soup and flour together; spoon over top. **Do not stir.** Cover and cook on high 3 to 3½ hours or on low 6 to 8 hours or until chicken and vegetables are tender. Serve on a bed of rice or noodles.

MAKE-AHEAD CHICKEN DINNER

1 chicken, cut up
3 tsp. basil
2 tsp. thyme
3 tsp. parsley
3 tsp. tarragon
2 tsp. sage

1-2 jars whole mushrooms,
  drained
1 pkg. peas
1½-2 c. orange juice
Salt & pepper to taste
White wine

Place all ingredients, except white wine, in crockpot. Cook on high until chicken is done. Turn to low. May add white wine for extra liquid, if desired. Serve over rice or noodles.

SPANISH CHICKEN

3 to 4-lb. chicken, cut up
Salt, pepper & paprika to taste
Garlic salt (opt.)
1 (6-oz.) can tomato paste

½ can beer (6 oz.)
1 sm. jar stuffed olives with ¾
  c. liquid

Season washed and cut-up chicken with salt, pepper, paprika and garlic salt, if desired. Place in crockpot. Mix tomato paste and beer together and pour over chicken. Add olives. Cover and cook on low 7 to 9 hours. Serve over rice or noodles.

CHICKEN LIVERS & RICE

1 lb. chicken livers
½ c. flour
1 tsp. salt
¼ tsp. pepper
3 slices bacon, diced
3 green onions with tops,
  chopped

1 c. chicken bouillon
1 (10-oz.) can golden mushroom
  soup
1 (4-oz.) can sliced mushrooms,
  drained
¼ c. dry white wine

Cut chicken livers into bite-sized pieces. Toss in flour, salt and pepper. Fry bacon pieces in large skillet. Remove when brown, reserving grease. Add flour-coated chicken livers and green onion to bacon grease in skillet; sauté until lightly browned. Pour chicken bouillon into skillet; stir into drippings. Pour all into crockpot. Add browned bacon bits, soup, mushrooms and wine. Cover and cook on low 4 to 6 hours. Serve over rice, toast or buttered noodles.

CHICKEN CACCIATORE

2 med. onions, sliced
2½ to 3-lb. chicken, cut up
2 cloves garlic, minced
1 (1-lb.) can tomatoes
1 (8-oz.) can tomato sauce
1 tsp. salt

¼ tsp. pepper
1-2 oregano leaves, crushed
½ tsp. basil, crushed
½ tsp. celery seed
1 bay leaf

Place onions in bottom of crockpot. Add chicken pieces and remaining ingredients. Cover and cook on low 6 to 8 hours or on high 2½ to 4 hours. Serve chicken with sauce over hot-buttered spaghetti or rice.

CHICKEN 'N NOODLES

4 c. chicken broth
5-6 c. noodles
Salt to taste

1 (3 to 4-lb.) cooked chicken,
   cut up

Put chicken broth in crockpot. Salt and pepper to taste. Turn crockpot on high and cook broth until boiling. Add noodles; stir well and cover. Cook 30 to 45 minutes, stirring occasionally. Serve with chicken.

EASY CHICKEN CACCIATORE (EASY)

2 onions, sliced thin
4 med. carrots, sliced

4 chicken breasts
1 (32-oz.) jar spaghetti sauce

Place sliced onions and carrots in bottom of crockpot. Add chicken breasts. Pour spaghetti sauce over chicken. Cook on low 8 hours. Serve chicken with sauce over spaghetti noodles.

CHICKEN ITALIANO (EASY)

Skinned chicken breasts
1 (8-oz.) can tomato sauce

1 env. spaghetti sauce mix
1 c. water
1 (4-oz.) can mushrooms

Place enough skinned chicken breasts in crockpot to cover bottom. Combine tomato sauce, sauce mix, water and mushrooms. Pour over chicken in crockpot. Cook on high approximately 5 hours or until done. Serve with spaghetti noodles.

CHICKEN PARMIGIANA

1 egg
1 tsp. salt
¼ tsp. pepper
3 boneless chicken breasts or 6
  halves

1 c. bread crumbs
½ c. butter
1 sm. eggplant in slices (opt.)
1 (10½-oz.) can pizza sauce
6 slices mozzarella cheese

In bowl beat egg, salt and pepper. Dip chicken into mixture, then into bread crumbs. Sauté chicken in the butter until lightly brown. Arrange chicken and eggplant in bottom of crockpot. Pour pizza sauce over chicken. Cook 6 to 8 hours on low. Top with mozzarella cheese and bake an additional 15 minutes. Serve with any type of pasta.

CHICKEN TETRAZZINI WITH HAM

1½ c. chicken broth
1½ c. water
1 c. chicken, cooked and cubed
2 c. cooked spaghetti, broken
  into 2-in. pieces
1 can cream of chicken soup

1 c. light cream
1 c. ham, cooked & cubed
1 (4-oz.) can drained
  mushrooms
¼ c. grated Parmesan cheese
2 T. parsley

Combine all ingredients except cheese and parsley. Cook in crockpot several hours to let flavors blend. Serve with cheese and parsley on top.

CHICKEN TETRAZZINI

2-3 c. chicken, cooked & diced
2 c. chicken broth
1 sm. onion, finely chopped
¼ c. milk
¼ c. slivered almonds (opt.)

2 (4-oz.) cans sliced
  mushrooms, drained
1 can cream of mushroom soup
Parmesan cheese
Spaghetti

Combine all ingredients except Parmesan cheese and spaghetti in crockpot. Cover and cook on high 1 hour, then on low 6 to 8 hours. Serve over buttered spaghetti and sprinkle generously with Parmesan cheese.

CHEESY CHICKEN QUICHE

2 T. corn oil
2 lbs. chicken breasts,
  boneless & skinless
¾ c. flour
¾ tsp. baking powder
½ tsp. salt

1 c. evaporated milk
2 eggs, beaten
1 c. cheddar cheese, shredded
2 T. onion, chopped
2 tsp. dried parsley flakes

Coat crockpot with corn oil. Cook chicken on low 6 to 8 hours or on high 3 to 4 hours or until tender. Stir together flour, baking powder, salt, milk and eggs, then fold in cheese, onion and parsley. Pour mixture over chicken and cook 1 hour on high.

TURKEY

TURKEY DIVAN (EASY)

2-3 c. turkey, cooked, cut-up
½ sm. onion, diced
1 can condensed cream of
  chicken soup
½ c. mayonnaise
3 T. flour

2 stalks celery, sliced
1 (10-oz.) pkg. frozen broccoli
  pieces
1 tsp. curry powder
1 T. lemon juice

Combine all ingredients. Pour into lightly greased crockpot. Cook on low 6 to 8 hours or on high 2 to 3 hours. Serve over hot, buttered noodles.

CORN & TURKEY CASSEROLE

1 T. margarine
1 onion, chopped
1 (16-oz.) can cream-style corn
4 lg. eggs
½ c. evaporated milk
⅓ c. all-purpose flour

Salt to taste
Black pepper to taste
2 c. turkey, cooked & chopped
1 c. mild or sharp cheddar
  cheese, shredded

In a skillet melt margarine over medium heat. Add chopped onion and cook until softened, about 5 minutes. Transfer to medium-sized mixing bowl. Whisk creamed corn, eggs, evaporated milk, flour, salt and pepper into onion. Stir in chopped turkey. Transfer to lightly greased crockpot. Cover and cook on high 2½ to 3 hours or until knife inserted comes out clean. Sprinkle top of casserole with cheese. Cover and cook until cheese is melted, about 15 minutes. Serve immediately.

TURKEY & TOMATOEY PASTA

3 (14-oz.) cans diced tomatoes
2 tsp. chili powder
½ tsp. garlic powder

1 c. turkey, cooked & cubed
1 (8-oz.) uncooked spiral pasta

Mix together tomatoes, chili powder, garlic powder and turkey in crock-pot. Turn on high and let mixture heat through, approximately 1 to 1½ hours. Once mixture is heated, stir in uncooked pasta. Cook for an additional 30 minutes to 1 hour until pasta is tender.

OLÉ TURKEY (EASY)

4 c. turkey, cooked & shredded
1 (1⅝-oz.) pkg. enchilada sauce
  mix
2 (6-oz.) cans tomato paste
½ c. water

1 c. Monterey Jack cheese,
  shredded
Corn chips or rice
Garnish: sour cream, sliced
  green onions, sliced ripe olives

Stir shredded turkey, enchilada sauce mix, tomato paste and water into crockpot. Cover; cook on low 7 to 8 hours or on high 3 to 4 hours. If on low, turn to high and add cheese. Allow cheese to melt. Serve with corn chips or rice. Delicious also as a filling for tacos or tostadas.

PHEASANT

TENDER PHEASANT

Flour
1 pheasant, cleaned, washed &
  cut in pieces as a fryer
Salt & pepper to taste

½ c. butter
2 onions, thinly sliced
½ c. water

Flour pheasant lightly; sprinkle with salt and pepper. Slice half of butter into bottom of crockpot. Cover with thin layer of onions. Arrange pheasant pieces over onion; cover with remaining onions. Dot with remaining butter. Add water. Cover and cook on low 4 to 5 hours.

CREAMY PHEASANT

6-7 cans cream soups (do not
  add water)
Carrots, sliced or chopped
Celery, chopped
Browned bite-sized pieces of
  pheasant (3-4 birds)

Mushrooms
Water chestnuts
Bamboo shoots
Steamed broccoli
Steamed rice

Combine soups, carrots, celery and pheasant in crockpot. Let simmer on low 4 to 6 hours. 30 minutes before serving, add mushrooms, canned water chestnuts and bamboo shoots. Float broccoli on top and serve over wild rice or plain or brown rice.

SLOW COOKED SAUCES

SAUCES

HOMESTYLE SPAGHETTI SAUCE

¾ lb. lean ground beef or
  ground turkey
2 cloves garlic, crushed
½ lg. onion, diced
1 stalk celery, diced
1 c. whole fresh mushrooms
¼ c. fresh parsley, chopped
1 tsp. Italian seasoning

1 (28-oz.) can whole tomatoes,
  undrained
1 (6-oz.) can tomato paste
¼ c. dry red wine
1 T. sugar
½ T. salt
½ tsp. black pepper

Break up beef in a large crockpot, then add remaining ingredients. Stir to blend well, then cover and cook on high 4 to 6 hours or low 8 to 10 hours. For thicker sauce, uncover for final 1 to 2 hours of cooking.

DELICIOUS SPAGHETTI SAUCE

1 lb. ground beef
1 can tomato soup
1 can tomato sauce
1 can mushroom soup
1 stick pepperoni, sliced
Black olives, sliced

1 can mushrooms (stems &
pieces)
2 tsp. mustard
2 tsp. Italian seasoning
Bay leaf

Brown beef. Place beef and remaining ingredients in crockpot and simmer 8 to 10 hours.

CROCKPOT CHILI VERDE

½ lb. pork, browned & cubed
½ c. water
Garlic & cumin to taste
2 cans tomatoes, diced (No. 2½ can)

1 lg. can tomato sauce or 1 lg.
can hot sauce
2 cans chilies, diced
1 can mushrooms
1 can olives, sliced

Combine all ingredients and simmer in crockpot all day on low. Serve over burritos or other Mexican foods. Makes a large batch and can be frozen for later.

MUSHROOM-CHICKEN PASTA SAUCE

2 to 3-lb. fryer, whole or cut up
2 stalks celery, sliced
2 onions, chopped
1 tsp. salt
½ c. chicken broth or water
1 (6-oz.) can tomato paste
¼ c. dry sherry
1 tsp. oregano

1 lb. mushrooms, sliced or 2
cans sliced mushrooms,
drained
2 T. butter
2 T. flour
½ c. heavy cream or half & half

Place fryer in crockpot with celery, onions and salt. Combine chicken broth with tomato paste and pour over ingredients in crockpot. Add sherry, oregano and mushrooms; stir to moisten all ingredients. Cover and cook on low 8 to 10 hours or on high 3½ to 5 hours. Remove chicken; bone meat and dice. Return meat to crockpot. Knead butter and flour together and add with cream; stir well. Cover and cook on high ½ to 1½ hours or on low 3 to 5 hours.

CROCK-98

BARBECUE SAUCE

2 T. butter
1 onion, diced
1 clove garlic (opt.)
½ c. celery, chopped
¾ c. water (off roast)
1 c. ketchup
2 T. vinegar

2 T. lemon juice
2 T. Worcestershire sauce
2 T. brown sugar
1 tsp. dry mustard
1 tsp. soda
¼ tsp. pepper

Melt butter in saucepan. Add onion and cook until browned. Add remaining ingredients and simmer about 20 minutes. Transfer all ingredients to crockpot and simmer on low 4 to 6 hours.

CROCK BARBECUE SAUCE

1 c. ketchup
1 T. Worcestershire sauce
2-3 drops tabasco pepper sauce
1 c. water

¼ c. vinegar
1 T. brown sugar
1 tsp. salt
1 tsp. celery seed
1 T. instant minced onion

Combine all ingredients in crockpot. Cook on low 2 to 3 hours.

KETCHUP

1 gal. tomatoes
⅔ c. onions, chopped
1½ c. sugar
1 tsp. nutmeg
¾ tsp. tabasco pepper sauce
½ tsp. curry powder

2 c. vinegar
1 tsp. dry mustard
5 tsp. salt
2 tsp. ginger
1 tsp. cinnamon
2 apples

Skin tomatoes and cook until soft. Blend or use food processor. Add all other ingredients and cook overnight in crockpot.

CROCKPOT APPLE BUTTER (EASY)

8 c. apple pulp
2½ tsp. cinnamon
¼ tsp. allspice

4 c. sugar
½ tsp. nutmeg

Put all ingredients in crockpot. Cook on high 3 to 4 hours, then on low 2 to 3 hours. (Cover may be removed last hour of cooking for a thicker butter.) Stir every 2 hours. Ladle in hot sterilized jars. Makes 6 pints.

SIMMERED SWEETS

DESSERTS

INDIAN PUDDING

3 c. milk
½ c. cornmeal
½ tsp. salt
3 eggs

¼ c. sugar
⅓ c. molasses
½ tsp. ginger
½ tsp. cinnamon

Lightly grease crockpot and preheat on high. Bring milk, cornmeal and salt to boil in saucepan. Stirring constantly, boil 5 minutes. Cover and simmer 10 minutes. In large bowl combine eggs, sugar, molasses, ginger and cinnamon. Gradually beat in hot cornmeal mixture with electric mixer. Pour into crockpot. Cover and cook on high 2 to 3 hours, or on low 6 to 8 hours. **Variation:** Add ½ cup raisins and chopped apples to a doubled recipe.

STEAMED MINCEMEAT PUDDING

½ c. butter, soft
1 c. granulated sugar
2 eggs
1¾ c. sifted flour
2 tsp. baking powder

1 tsp. salt
½ tsp. cinnamon
⅔ c. evaporated milk
1 tsp. rum extract (opt.)
1½ c. prepared mincemeat

Cream butter and sugar until light. Add eggs, beating thoroughly after each. Sift dry ingredients and add alternately with milk, beating until smooth. Stir in rum extract. Stir in mincemeat. Pour into greased 1½-quart mold or 2-pound coffee can. Place in crockpot and cook on low 8 to 10 hours. Serve with Orange-Honey Hard Sauce.

Orange-Honey Hard Sauce:

½ c. soft margarine
3 T. honey

1 tsp. grated orange rind
1½ c. confectioners' sugar

Beat all ingredients together until light. To make flame pudding, top pudding with sauce and add sugar cube saturated with lemon extract. When serving, light the cube.

PEARS IN RICE PUDDING

4 c. lite evaporated milk
¾ c. sugar
½ c. short grain rice, cooked
1 T. cornstarch
2 eggs, beaten

1 (16-oz.) can pears, drained & chopped
1½ tsp. vanilla extract
1 T. brown sugar
½ tsp. ground cinnamon

Lightly grease crockpot. In mixing bowl combine evaporated milk, sugar and rice. Stir in cornstarch. Gradually add beaten eggs. Fold in pears and vanilla. Pour into crockpot. Combine brown sugar and cinnamon in small bowl. Sprinkle over the rice mixture. Cover and cook 2 to 3 hours or until pudding is set. Serve.

POACHED PEARS IN RED WINE

2 c. port or dry red wine
2 c. sugar
6-8 med. ripe pears, pared

Red food coloring
4 thin strips lemon peel

Put wine and sugar in crockpot. Cover and cook on high until sugar is dissolved. Peel pears, keeping them whole and leaving stems on. Put in crockpot, turning to coat well. Add food coloring and lemon peel. Cover and cook on low 4 to 6 hours, turning occasionally to coat with wine mixture. Serve with wine sauce poured over pears.

SLOW COOKED APPLES

6-8 baking apples, washed &
   cored, with top 1/3 of apple
   pared
1 c. raisins
1 c. pecans, chopped

1 c. brown sugar
1 tsp. cinnamon
1/2 tsp. nutmeg
2 T. butter
1/2 c. water

Place apples in crockpot. Mix raisins, pecans and sugar together and fill apples with it. Sprinkle with cinnamon and nutmeg. Dot with butter. Add water; cover and cook on low 8 hours or overnight.

DELICIOUS APPLE CAKE

2 c. sugar
1 c. oil
2 eggs
2 tsp. vanilla
2 c. flour
1 tsp. salt

1 tsp. soda
1 tsp. nutmeg
2 c. Delicious apples, finely
   chopped & not pared
1 c. black walnuts, chopped

Beat sugar, oil and eggs together well. Add vanilla. Sift flour, salt, soda and nutmeg together. Add chopped apples to sugar mixture and beat well. Stir in flour mixture and nuts; mix well. Pour batter into greased and floured 2-pound coffee can. Place in crockpot and bake until set.

SPICED CARROT CAKE

2½ c. flour
2½ c. sugar
1½ tsp. baking powder
½ tsp. soda
¼ tsp. salt
1 tsp. nutmeg
1 tsp. cinnamon
½ tsp. ground cloves

1½ c. raw carrots (4-5 carrots),
  grated
1½ c. salad oil
4 eggs
¼ c. hot water
1 c. nuts, chopped
1 c. raisins (opt.)

Stir together flour, sugar, baking powder, soda, salt, nutmeg, cinnamon and cloves. Grate carrots to a fine consistency. In large bowl beat oil and eggs together. Add hot water and continue to beat. Stir in grated carrots. Add flour mixture, nuts and raisins; mix together thoroughly. Turn batter into greased and floured 3-pound coffee can or 2½-quart mold. Place in crockpot and bake 3½ to 4 hours on high.

FRUIT COBBLER

1 batch biscuit mix drop
  biscuits (approx. 9)
¼ c. brown sugar (or more)

½ stick butter (or more)
1 tsp. cinnamon (or more)
2 lg. cans fruit pie filling

Make and bake biscuits per package directions; let cool. Combine brown sugar, butter and cinnamon in bowl or cup. Crumble biscuits into chunks. In large crockpot layer, starting with pie filling, then biscuits, then sugar. Repeat. Cook in crockpot until top bubbles. Can be made the night before and refrigerated until ready to cook.

CARAMEL NUT ROLLS

2 pkgs. refrigerator biscuits
1 c. brown sugar
½ c. nuts, chopped

½ c. melted butter or margarine
Cinnamon

Turn crockpot to high while preparing rolls. Mix brown sugar and nuts together. Dip each refrigerator biscuit in melted butter, then brown sugar and nuts. Place in well-greased 2-pound coffee can. Sprinkle each layer of biscuits with cinnamon. Place in crockpot and bake 3⅓ hours on low. **Variation:** Yeast rolls (frozen, unbaked) may be substituted for refrigerator biscuits. Fill can with dipped rolls and let rise before baking. Bake as directed 3 to 4 hours on low.

CROCK-98

DRIED FRUITS (EASY)

Place dried fruit in crockpot. Add the minimum water directed on dried fruit package. Cover and cook on low overnight. Serve warm with sour cream and dash of nutmeg.

DESSERT FONDUE

6 (1-oz.) squares unsweetened
  or semi-sweet chocolate
1½ c. sugar
½ c. butter or margarine

⅛ tsp. salt
3 T. creme de cocoa, rum or
  orange-flavored liqueur
¼ c. milk or cream

Put all ingredients in crockpot. Stir together thoroughly. Cover and set to high for 30 minutes. Stir well and set on low 2 to 6 hours. **Dessert Fondue Dippers:** Angel food cake, pound cake, marshmallows, apples, banana (cut in bite size pieces).

CARAMEL APPLE DIP (EASY)

1 can sweetened condensed
  milk
2 c. brown sugar, packed

½ c. butter
¾ c. white corn syrup
Pinch of salt

Bring all ingredients to boil, then boil and stir constantly for 5 minutes more. The mixture can be used for taffy apples or kept warm in crockpot or fondue pot and used for dipping sliced apples.

INDEX OF RECIPES

BEEF COOKERY

SLOW COOKED SAUCES

SAUCES

SIMMERED SWEETS

DESSERTS

How To Order

Crockery Cooking is the perfect gift for cooks and cookbook collectors. If you would like to order additional copies, please return an order form with your check or money order to:

Crockery Cooking
Morris Press Cookbooks – Retail Sales
P.O. Box 2110
Kearney, NE 68848

Please mail me ___ copies of *Crockery Cooking* at $5.95 per copy and $2.00 for shipping and handling for each book.* I have enclosed my check/money order (made payable to Morris Press Cookbooks) in the amount of $_____.
Mail my books to: (please type or print clearly)

Name_____

Address_____

City_____State_____ Zip_____
* NE residents add 5% state sales tax and any local tax to your total order.

Please mail me ___ copies of *Crockery Cooking* at $5.95 per copy and $2.00 for shipping and handling for each book.* I have enclosed my check/money order (made payable to Morris Press Cookbooks) in the amount of $_____.
Mail my books to: (please type or print clearly)

Name_____

Address_____

City_____State_____ Zip_____
* NE residents add 5% state sales tax and any local tax to your total order.

Please mail me ___ copies of *Crockery Cooking* at $5.95 per copy and $2.00 for shipping and handling for each book.* I have enclosed my check/money order (made payable to Morris Press Cookbooks) in the amount of $_____.
Mail my books to: (please type or print clearly)

Name_____

Address_____

City_____State_____ Zip_____
* NE residents add 5% state sales tax and any local tax to your total order.

PUBLISH YOUR OWN *Cookbook*

Churches, schools, organizations, families, and businesses can preserve their favorite recipes by publishing a custom cookbook. Cookbooks make a great **fundraiser** because they are easy to sell and highly profitable. Our low prices also make cookbooks a perfect affordable **keepsake**. We offer:

- Low prices, high quality, and prompt service.
- Many options and styles to suit your needs.
- 90 days to pay and a written No-Risk Guarantee.

Order our FREE Cookbook Kit for full details:

- Call us at **800-445-6621, ext. CB**.
- Visit our web site at **www.morriscookbooks.com**.
- Mail the **postage-paid reply card** below.

✂ -

ALL THE INGREDIENTS FOR SUCCESS!™

Order our **FREE** Cookbook Kit. Please print neatly.

Name _____

Organization _____

Address_____

City _____ State _____ Zip _____

E-mail _____

Phone (_____) _____

Back Card 2-12

P. O. Box 2110
Kearney, NE 68848

MORRIS PRESS COOKBOOKS

PUBLISH
YOUR OWN
Cookbook

Whether your goal is to raise funds or create a cherished keepsake, Morris Press Cookbooks has all the right ingredients to make a great custom cookbook. Raise **$500 – $50,000** or more while preserving favorite recipes.

Three ways to order our **FREE** Cookbook Kit:
- Call us at **800-445-6621, ext. CB**.
- Visit our web site at **www.morriscookbooks.com**.
- Complete and mail the **reply card** below.

ALL THE INGREDIENTS
FOR SUCCESS!™

Use your smart phone
QR app to learn more.